Blitzkrieg Bops

Published by 404 Ink Limited
www.404Ink.com
@404Ink

Editing & proofreading: Heather McDaid
Typesetting: Laura Jones-Rivera
Cover design: Luke Bird
Co-founders and publishers of 404 Ink:
Heather McDaid & Laura Jones-Rivera

Print ISBN: 978-1-912489-90-9
Ebook ISBN: 978-1-912489-91-6

Printed and bound in Great Britain by Clays Ltd, Elcograf S.p.A.

MIX
Paper | Supporting
responsible forestry
FSC
www.fsc.org
FSC® C018072

404 Ink acknowledges and is thankful for support from Creative Scotland in the publication of this title.

ALBA | CHRUTHACHAIL

LOTTERY FUNDED

Blitzkrieg Bops

A Brief History of Punks at War

Alli Patton

Inklings

Contents

Playlist

If you're looking for the perfect soundtrack to the book, you can listen to Alli's 'Blitzkrieg Bops' playlist on You-Tube, by using the QR code below or go to rb.gy/b2t4d6.

Enjoy.

Introduction

Frenzied and furious, strings thrash like bullets ripping through the air. A barrage of drumbeats hit like heavy boots to soil. Through the roar of sound and fury, a distant voice cries out like orders in battle. With each blistering note, the bullets fly, the tanks roll out, the feet march on, and the blitzkrieg bops.

Since its inception, punk music and its subculture have defied convention, first emerging from a profound aversion to all things mainstream. Angry, unruly, and equipped with an "anti" ethos – aggressively anti-establishment, anti-authoritarian, anti-corporation, and anti-conformity – punk became a rebellion bound in leather, secured by safety pins, and informed by an innately anarchic resolve.

Exploding almost simultaneously in New York and London in the mid-1970s, early punk musicians traded in the polished, often excessive stylings of popular rock for a rougher, more stripped-down approach, resulting in the genre's quintessential sound: a cacophony of shouted vocals, snarled chords, and distorted notes soundtracked this youth crusade, a cause among the alienated and enraged.

Punk predecessors examined society and culture through fuck-you-tinted glasses, crafting songs meant to ignite collective rage using blunt, socially charged lyrics. Many of the genre's English forebears deployed their combative rock to critique the monarchy, aristocracy, and working-class life. Their U.S. counterparts were more fueled by angst, liberating listeners from American ideals by bashing their parents' middle-class values and prophesying the evils of suburban conformity.

In the United Kingdom, nihilistic tyrants the Sex Pistols may have initially sparked the punk flame, but The Clash – most famously made up of Joe Strummer, Mick Jones, Paul Simonon and Nicky "Topper" Headon – fed it, their politically bent lyrics and commitment to social justice setting an early precedent. Their socially conscious songs addressed issues that plagued their London home, like poverty and inequality, but they did so by, at times, implementing images of war and insurrection. While The Clash held a staunchly anti-war outlook, perhaps by viewing these societal struggles through a war-warped lens, the band attempted to emphasize their gravity. "White Riot", for instance, sounds like calls for a violent uprising; in reality, the shouted anthem decried apathy among the day's white citizens and their passivity toward the oppression happening around them. Born from witnessing the Notting Hill Carnival riots of 1976 – in which the Black community of West London's prolonged struggles with over-policing, harassment and brutality came to a head during the district-wide cultural celebration[1] – the song urged white youth to take a stand against the establishment too.[2] Songs like "Straight to Hell" and "Atom Tan" have always, to me, planted listeners amid conflict as the band uses the aftermath of the Vietnam War and threat of nuclear warfare respectively as vehicles for examining complex topics like immigration and identity to media-induced paranoia or the rising entertainment value of televised destruction.

The Ramones – formed in 1974 in Queens, New York – embraced similar imagery in their overall aesthetic, masquerading as a unit, the foot soldiers of a burgeoning punk army, with Joey, Dee Dee, Johnny, Tommy and members thereafter adopting the Ramone surname. While some early punks donned symbols like swastikas as a means of provocation, they preferred fatigues of ripped jeans and leather jackets. Even still, "Blitzkrieg Bop" – their classic opus from which this book takes its name – references the military tactic, blitzkrieg, or "lightning war", a method of offensive warfare seeking to defeat opponents in a series of short but violent surprise attacks, in what would become a rallying cry among their fans.

War became an effective tool for many punks; employing symbols of brutality and strife made their messages and issues all the more urgent. These early punks undoubtedly started a cultural revolution, but one in which combat was chic and militancy was trendy. Their music left an indelible mark, but the punks who have endured these real-life hostilities have never needed to borrow such theatrics: they've lived them.

Like some of these aforementioned punks, I, too, have never had to survive amidst war or exist under brutal authoritarian rule like those within these pages. I grew up deep in the American South, where my experience was shaped by privilege because of the color of my skin while others have faced systemic discrimination because of theirs.

Growing up in Alabama, an epicenter of the civil rights movement that saw people mobilized against racial segregation and discrimination throughout the 1950s and '60s, I learned of the freedom songs that became vital to the movement. "We Shall Overcome", "We Shall Not Be Moved", "Everybody Wants Freedom" – songs like these inspired bravery, unity and hope among demonstrators who were often met with violence in their fight for equality. In learning about the power of these songs and the courage of those who sang them, I realized music had the capacity to be more than just sounds; it could bring people together, spark revolution. I became fascinated by the genres that channeled this push for change and by those who protested, who stood for – and against – something through music.

When artillery blasts and rifle fire become the backdrop to your everyday, it's one thing to fight the establishment; it's another to fight for your life. I will never personally understand what it's like to experience animosity for simply existing or fathom the immense hardships many have had to endure. I am, however, committed to honoring and sharing the stories of those who have used music's transformative power to stand up for what they believe in.

Generations of punks have done so, a striking example emerging in Death Pill, the all-female Ukrainian punk outfit. In March 2022, the trio, comprising lead vocalist and guitarist Mariana Navrotskaya, bassist Natalya Seryakova, and drummer Anastasiya Khomenko, released "Расцарапаю Ебало", which translates as "Scratch Asshole",[3] the accompanying Bandcamp message reading: "We dedicate this release to everyone who defends our country. We are ready to tear the face of every freak who encroaches on our freedom and independence with our manicured nails."

With the same sobering intensity of their promise, the song gnashes at the ears and claws for the heart. The ferocity of the piercing vocals and the persistence of the battering beat echo the band's new reality, mirroring the missile strikes, military attacks, and unrelenting siege that became their lives overnight.

Weeks prior, Russia's President Vladimir Putin announced a "special military operation", propagandizing the need "to protect people who have been subjected to abuse and genocide by the Kyiv regime",[4] launching a full-scale invasion of their country, and masking his own ambitions for control of the region. Forces, under Putin's orders, spilled into neighboring Ukraine from the east, targeting locations near the nation's capital of Kyiv. "When you're hearing all these explosions, all these shootings, you really don't know if you will wake up in the morning," explains Death Pill's Khomenko. When we spoke, the conflict was still ravaging their country.

The trio was completing their debut album when the war began. Despite their new reality, they carried on, remastering each previously recorded track to mirror their newborn rage. What began as a rejection of societal pressures forced on young women grew into a stirring oeuvre of strength and resilience.

"Расцарапаю Ебало", once filled with bite reserved explicitly for an ex-boyfriend, transformed into a pointed message to oppressors, threats to "Scratch your face to fucking blood!" meeting the ear with renewed severity. "Dirty Rotten Youth", an ominous death march through adolescence, felt even more fury-tinged, proclaiming, "Useless pale life – this is only your choice." The lyrics of their stinging feminist hymn, "Go Your Way", grew all the more urgent, cries to "Fight for your respect" ringing out over the frenzied composition, while the vicious anthem "Die for Vietnam" turned all too real amid thrashing strings and visceral wails, warning, "Beware! Napalm's everywhere!" Their album was released one year after the invasion and has since been re-released with all Russian-language lyrics removed.

As they toured across Europe and the United Kingdom in 2023, they did so with the Ukrainian flag duct taped proudly behind them at every gig. Death Pill's searing songs became so much more. On stage, they exploded into powerful messages of resistance, with fans shouting "Slava Ukraini" or "Glory to Ukraine".

Throughout, Death Pill used their music to raise money for Ukrainian armed forces. "They have to kill people," explains Khomenko of their fellow punks on the frontline. "They have to survive. They have to go through really, really difficult things, and I hate it so fucking much."

"Now, I hope that all the world realizes what is actually bad, and who is really evil," notes their bassist. "It's not punk rockers."

Over six million Ukrainians have since been displaced, seeking refuge within the battle-scarred region and beyond;[5] loved ones have been forced to part ways; and the members of Death Pill were not exempt from such separation.

Khomenko fled to Spain, taking her young son, mother, and nephew to Barcelona. Seryakova found refuge in Australia, settling on the southern coast in Adelaide. Navrotskaya remained in Kyiv, a place that initially avoided Russian seizure but has since faced several attacks. As I write, over two years on, Kyiv just sustained bombardment of its energy infrastructure, Russian missiles having damaged DTEK thermal power plants.[6] The war remains ongoing.

Since the dawn of the genre, many bands like Death Pill have chosen to live courageously in times of conflict. Theirs join the multitude of stories in which punks have used their music as a life preserver, turning mere songs into shouts of activism and platforms for change. This book is about those punks. It is also for them.

Blitzkrieg Bops offers a brief history of punks at war, a snapshot across decades, continents, and cultures to understand how they've used their craft as a means of resistance and resilience, in the name of change. Rife with stories of those who have soundtracked movements, wielded their music as a daring fist in the face of unimaginable violence, against corrupt governments and tyrannical regimes, this book invites you to bear witness to the reality of what it means to turn to art for survival, when lives and freedoms are on the line. Through these conversations, I hope to illustrate not only the impact of music in times of extreme crisis, but the need for a defiant voice, when an oppressive one is the loudest in the room. I ask, in turn, that you consider the power of these punks' protests and how their efforts, how these movements can be amplified by us all as many of them – and many more punks to come – continue to fight.

This is *Blitzkrieg Bops*. These are punks at war.

Chapter 1

1970s: Dancing on the Corpse of Apartheid

Punk was born when it was needed most. While the 1970s are often stylized as an era awash in the silvery light of disco ball decadence, it was also marked by instability, which cast a bleak pall over both the United Kingdom and the United States.

After years of relative prosperity following the Second World War, the two Western nations experienced a combination of economic stagnation and rising inflation.[7] Where the cost of living spiked – food and energy prices accelerated dramatically – employment dwindled, with both nations seeing 5-6% of their labor forces out of work by 1979.[8] [9]

This economic turbulence stemmed from a revolving door of incidents like the 1973 oil crisis, in which the Organization of Arab Petroleum Exporting Countries implemented an oil embargo against those who supported Israel during the Fourth Arab-Israeli War,[10] and the subsequent 1979 energy crisis, where a roughly 7% drop in oil production in the wake of the Iranian revolution caused global knock-on impacts.[11] Labor strikes were frequent, especially between coal miners and steel workers, as strains were felt from the move toward deindustrialization. The decade saw also dramatic changes in leadership. Where U.S. citizens saw faith tested with President Richard Nixon's resignation following the Watergate scandal, Britain saw Margaret Thatcher take the helm of the Conservative Party with numerous controversial policies.

The world was changing as the Vietnam War waged on and various movements sought to shape the future. Despite advancements made during the civil rights movement, Black citizens continued their fight against discrimination, especially in the workforce and education.[12] The Stonewall Riots of 1969 stirred greater political activism for LGBTQ+ rights, leading to the formation of global organizations, like the Gay Liberation Front and the Gay Activist Alliance.[13] During this time, women demanded equal pay, an end to employment discrimination and autonomy over their bodies and reproductive rights.[14] There was promise of change on the horizon, however, that promise was often met with disillusionment over this surmounting inequality in regards to race, class, sexuality, and gender.

Punk music would become the perfect outlet for the era's youth to roar their discontent. Flinging their frustrations at authority and the establishment, punks created their own social and political commentary through music. Struggling with the imposing classism? The Sex Pistols called for "Anarchy in the U.K.". Feeling alienated by society? The Ramones commiserated with "Teenage Lobotomy". Pointed songs and abrasive style was used to upend the norm, making collective hardships more bearable.

It wouldn't be long before punk transcended into a global countercultural phenomenon. It crossed the U.S., adding to its roster Los Angeles-based icons X and the Germs, enduring Latino and Chicano acts like The Zeros and Los Illegals, and Bay Area hardcore stalwarts the Dead Kennedys. Punk also made its way to Japan early on, with Tokyo nurturing a vibrant local scene thanks to venues like Shinjuku-Loft and S-Ken Studio. It sunk its teeth in Australia, where Queensland punks The Saints emerged against the strict right-wing rule of Johannes Bjelke-Petersen, helping to forge a continent-wide scene that would give life to bands like Perth's The Scientists and Melbourne art punks The Boys Next Door, some of whom would go on to form Nick Cave and the Bad Seeds.[15] Punk music adapted to meet the demands and concerns of both musicians and fans worldwide during their own times of need, becoming a source of solace, solidarity or something far more severe.

When punk made its way to Northern Ireland in 1976, it did so against the backdrop of a country fractured by a decades-long sectarian conflict known as The Troubles. That year alone, the nation witnessed the Kingsmill Massacre, resulting in the deaths of ten Protestant men;[16] saw the Hillcrest Bar bombing end in four Catholic people murdered and over 50 more citizens injured;[17] and beheld the loss of 297 people to the brutality.[18]

Beginning in the late 1960s and lasting until the 1990s, the Troubles was a complex time marked by constant infighting and rampant terrorism. The bloody conflict pitted neighbor against neighbor, dividing the primarily Protestant Unionists who wanted to maintain Northern Ireland's ties to the United Kingdom from the predominantly Catholic Nationalists who sought to unite the region with the Republic of Ireland. Various paramilitary groups – like the mostly Unionist Ulster Volunteer Force and Ulster Defence Association, and the primarily Nationalist Irish Republican Army and Irish National Liberation Army, even the British army – played a part in carrying out the violence, through street fighting, rioting, and deploying tactics of guerilla warfare to further deepen the rift and advance respective political agendas.[19]

Amidst bitter violence, through bomb blasts and rifle fire, came a handful of bands who would ultimately unite the youth of this divided nation – a generation caught in the crossfire.

The spark of the punk movement ignited in Belfast, Northern Ireland's capital and an epicenter of the period's unrest. Local acts led the charge, such as cover band-turned-punks Rudi, anti-sectarians Ruefrex, the still-active Undertones in nearby Derry, and the most politically vocal of them all, Stiff Little Fingers.[20] These bands offered an escape – some semblance of community – when such a thing seemed scarce.

Reflecting on the years preceding The Troubles, Ali McMordie, longtime bassist of Stiff Little Fingers, recalls, "I remember in the '60s, there was a great sense of community in the street. We were just like latchkey kids. We were just running around, eight, nine years old, free, no parental guidance. It didn't even matter if you didn't make it home for dinner. You could just pop into a neighbor's house, and they would feed you. That massively disappeared come '68, '69."

Along with that community, many forms of nightlife and entertainment also vanished. Many pubs, cinemas, and venues became widely inaccessible due to abbreviated bus services, strict curfews, and the "peace lines" put in place to separate feuding communities.[21] McMordie remembers the early days, saying, "We were just a band, trying to play gigs, the same as any other band. Because there was no other entertainment, we were just providing our own."

Stiff Little Fingers – formed in 1977 and originally made up of McMordie, frontman Jake Burns, guitarist Henry Cluney, and drummer Brian Faloon – would play many of their earliest gigs in Belfast City Centre, a place that would become a haven for them and their peers. "We all tended to bond together through the music," McMordie explains. Whatever their affiliation – punks, mods, skins, casuals – they would set aside their slight musical differences to congregate, create, and perform, where denominations and political ties mostly fell away. "In the City Centre, all that disappeared, and you were pretty much safe."

A few pubs, like The Pound and The Harp, opened their doors to punks when many wouldn't. To some, punk was a dirty word; its devotees, with their shocking appearances and blistering attitudes, were seen as a threat – not only by the authorities but also by publicans and landlords, warned against hosting such raucous acts. The British media, which had evangelized the nascent genre as a harbinger of immorality, made its way to Northern Ireland and damned the country's budding punk activity. "We were jeered at, spat upon," the bassist recounts. Threats towards the band were not uncommon. "Authority figures treated us at best with suspicion and at worst with open hostility and aggression."

"It was a bizarre, mad situation, but looking back, I still have good memories about it, and I think the good memories are just from the fact that in the face of massive adversity, you find a sense of kindredship… In terms of living through the conflict, it's amazing what, as human beings, we can put up with. We just get on with our everyday lives, and the grotesquely abnormal becomes every day. You change your lifestyle to suit and just try and survive."

Stiff Little Fingers were among the most outspoken regarding their lives at the height of the Troubles. By their 1979 debut, *Inflammable Material*, the conflict had been waging for a decade, witnessing pivotal moments like Bloody Sunday, in which British troops opened fire on civil rights demonstrators in Derry, killing thirteen people,[22] and Belfast's Bloody Friday, in which 22 bombs were detonated in a 75-minute space, killing nine and wounding well over 100.[23] The 1970s alone would account for the loss of nearly half of the irregular war's total fatalities.[24] The band translated this grim reality into song.

They hammered their anger and frustration into "Alternative Ulster", a pulsating anthem about being a young person caught between warring factions; they urged for change in "State of Emergency", a vicious call to action rallying others to alter their situation and combat hatred, with pleas to "try to change your life that is no life at all." The explosive "Suspect Device" exposed the paradox of the conflict: stripping freedoms in the name of being free. With "Wasted Life", they decried an existence of death and destruction with each bitter shriek.

"Killing isn't my idea of fun," they sneered on the track, noting that they wouldn't be a soldier in this madness with a cry of: "Stuff their fucking armies."

Weaving the Troubles into their music proved controversial, and Stiff Little Fingers faced opposition from fellow punks who felt their lyrics exploited the conflict. Where some challenged their oppressive environment, others sang as if they weren't living in one.

The Undertones, particularly, avoided the conflict in their music, instead writing songs that offered escape. Hits like "Jimmy Jimmy" and "Teenage Kicks" celebrated youth, identifying with the woes of adolescence or the joys of young romance. The decision to not be political is, in its own sense, political: "We've experienced a lot. Bloody Sunday. Civil rights marches. I'm not saying that we had more of a reason to sing about the Troubles than Stiff Little Fingers, but we did have a front row view," guitarist Damian O'Neill told the *Telegraph*,[25] with vocalist Fergal Sharkey elsewhere noting, "People used to ask early on why we didn't write songs about the Troubles; we were doing our best to escape from it."[26]

McMordie, defending Stiff Little Fingers' music and the criticism faced, asserts, "We never saw it as cashing in. It was just, 'This happened to us.'" These bands' music became more than expressions of rage, anthems of angst, or tributes to adolescence. Their songs attempted to create a common ground where there wasn't one, whether seeking escapism, or grounding listeners on the frontlines.

At the time, Stiff Little Fingers didn't think their actions particularly courageous. By writing and performing their music, daring to hurl discontent and challenge the status quo, they were making sense of their lives amid violence. He explains, "We saw a lot of what we were doing as a protest against our environment, against the oppression that we were getting from all sides." Their music became a way of sharing, empathizing, and connecting with people just like them, navigating the same conflict. "They were protesting against their environment, against the crap that they had to deal with in their own areas."

Amidst their words of rage, their songs of protest, whispered hope. It took decades after the conflict ended for McMordie to fully realize how much hope their music instilled. While preparing for one of their biggest-ever Belfast shows, he walked through the crowded city centre that had once been a refuge to so many when it struck him.

"I started thinking about the songs that we'd be playing, and it occurred to me those songs were quite dangerous," he says. "I suddenly remembered what it had been like over 45 years previously when we first wrote the songs. They were very contentious, but I just felt we had to do it, and at least thousands of other people felt that this needed to be said... I hadn't thought about that for quite some time, and it really hit me: the importance of the songs, what they had meant to so many others, and also what they had meant in directing their lives."

The music that came out of Northern Ireland during the Troubles did more than simply score the chaos. In putting an equally irate and unruly soundtrack to the brutality that became their norm, these punks – whether openly decrying the conflict or crafting narratives outside of the violence – created lifelines. They offered solidarity, comfort, and maybe, in a way, peace, with McMordie saying, "I'd like to think that we sowed some positive seeds."

The spirit of these punks would live long beyond the 1998 signing of the Good Friday Agreement, bringing to an end the three-decades-long conflict that had killed more than 3,700 people, injuring more than 47,000.[27] Manifested in more than just the many "peace lines" still dividing some Protestant and Catholic neighborhoods, the era left behind a legacy of trauma with the region experiencing high suicide rates and persistent substance abuse issues.[28] [29] With Brexit-related policies complicating border arrangements, and threatening the hard-won peace agreements,[30] a new wave of punks have taken up the mantle of their predecessors.

Proving that even back in its infancy, punk knew no borders, the genre would continue its transcendence, arriving in another nation deeply scarred by division in the late 1970s.

The young punk movement invaded South Africa at a time of institutionalized racial segregation and discrimination known as apartheid. This period of legalized racism began following the National Party's election in 1948 and lasted throughout their reign into the early 1990s, and saw citizens classified into racial groups: "White", "Indian", "Coloured" (or mixed race), and "Black."

Under Apartheid, an Afrikaans word meaning to "separate" or "set apart",[31] millions of South Africans were forcibly relocated to designated reserves, or townships, and the government controlled where "non-white" citizens could live and work, while dictating their movements within the country. Black workers, often employed as manual laborers or domestic workers, were temporarily allowed in white areas, forced to carry passbooks, internal passports that determined where they could travel based on employment. Interactions between different racial groups were also heavily policed, and social integration was actively discouraged if not punished. Integrated schools were abolished, mixed race marriages were illegal, and many public spaces, like restaurants, cinemas, parks, bathrooms, even benches, were segregated.[32] [33]

While this oppressive institution was opposed domestically and internationally – the United Nations placing arms embargoes and oil sanctions, and anti-Apartheid movements appearing across countries – activism within South Africa faced brutal repression. Demonstrations against apartheid policy could turn violent if not deadly, with one earlier, tragic example being 1960's Sharpeville massacre. Calling for the abolition of the pass laws, thousands of Black citizens joined in a countrywide demonstration that resulted in the deaths of 69 and the wounding of 180 when police opened fire into the crowd near the Sharpeville township.

Amidst the ongoing hostility, music emerged as a potent form of protest,[34] with punk succinctly soundtracking defiance. Benjy Mudie, A&R Director for South Africa's WEA Records, noted in the 2012 documentary *Punk In Africa* that the style resonated greatly with the nation's adolescents, punk speaking to the frustration of Black youth living under dehumanizing oppression and resonating with white youth who clashed with mandatory military conscription that perpetuated senseless violence. Those two very different worlds would collide in one band: National Wake.

Formed in the late 1970s, the multiracial punk band's mere existence challenged the system, blurring racial lines that separated the country and forging connections across the chasm. Ivan Kadey, the band's guitarist, remembers growing up during Apartheid: "We were totally segregated. In the areas we lived as white kids, the only Black people around were servants, laborers, people in the service industries, maids, and postmen."

Before the birth of National Wake, Kadey was already crafting protest music while studying architecture at university. He was living in Johannesburg with his then-girlfriend, now-wife, actress and cinematographer Nadine Kadey, whose footage of the band would be widely used throughout projects depicting their legacy today. Together, they shared a communal house with other young people – often of different races, which at the time was illegal – many of whom were actively involved in underground anti-apartheid movements. "We refused to be conditioned by the rules of apartheid."

In the summer of 1976, when a deadly student-led protest erupted against the introduction of the Afrikaans language into non-white schools, something stirred within Kadey. "That was a real 'get up, stand up' moment: look at these kids, it's time to take up the fight," he told the *Guardian*.[35] In witnessing the bravery and the fortitude of those during what became known as the Soweto uprising, the young artist envisioned forming a band with more than music, but a message. For years, that band remained only a dream; however, he was resolute: "I knew the band was going to be a shout against the situation in South Africa."

According to Kadey, the county's underground alternative community had been dreaming of an integrated scene, and it was through National Wake's formation and music that a long-desired multiracial underground could be nurtured.

They formed in the late 1970s when Kadey met brothers Gary and Punka Khoza, a bassist and drummer, whose family had been forced into the Soweto township under apartheid rule. "We hit it off," Kadey said of their first time playing together. The three would soon be joined by guitarist Steve Moni. "It was like magic."

"We knew we were taking a chance, but there was a more liberal sort of feeling in the air," Kadey explains, detailing how the government's power began shifting, causing cracks in the apartheid's façade to further fracture. Around then, Prime Minister P.W. Botha had taken control of the National Party. "[Botha] was talking about the need to change, adapt or die. So, there was stuff in the air that was saying these guys were seeing the need to move on, and we took that opportunity."

While there was an initial air of apprehension, the band's mission overshadowed the unease. "There were forces around us that were surveilling us," Kadey says, "but there was a commitment to speaking truth to power." They also had an unshakable belief in their songs, messages, and ability to bring about change. "The music was exciting, powerful. The best part of it was just to get up and play the music, so the fear just fell away."

National Wake's music was an intoxicating medley that fused punk's unruly energy, funk's sturdy grooves, and reggae's unwavering soul. Their music set listeners free, muting the outside world under a barrage of cymbal crashes, frenzied strings, and impassioned voices. "It was dance music," Kadey remembers. "People would jive and dance and go crazy."

Beneath the rousing sounds, their fearless lyrics addressed the injustices of apartheid head-on: "Walk in Africa" confronted early colonists who first exploited the country and its people. The searing "International News" condemned state censorship, exposing the paradoxes of international media, decrying how events, such as the Angolan War of Independence, were presented in and out of South Africa. They took aim at the white supremacist guns-for-hire wreaking havoc in "Mercenaries", where the swaggering "Supaman" highlighted the band's promise to "keep on moving, keep on fighting." Their anthem "Wake of the Nation" – much like the group's very moniker – was a double entendre, serving as a wake-up call and a funeral song for apartheid. A common thread emerged: determination to see the system's demise. As Kadey eloquently puts it, "We used to talk about dancing on the corpse of apartheid."

The liberal feeling present at the band's inception, however, began to dissipate. "The sort of right wing of the government clamped down, and things just started getting heavier and heavier," recalls Kadey. Because of its inherently activist nature, punk faced significant challenges under the country's draconian rule – music banned, gigs raided. National Wake struggled even to perform.[36] Kadey recalls one incident where a venue refused to allow them to play upon discovering their integrated lineup: "We got up and played anyway, and they pulled the plug." Venues that catered to multiracial crowds let alone gave a punk band like National Wake a microphone risked losing their liquor licenses or worse. According to James Greene Jr. in *Brave Punk World*, entire clubs could be teargassed and musicians arrested if either were suspected of engaging in anything resembling anti-apartheid activism.[37]

Their Johannesburg commune became a haven for National Wake and an unlikely refuge for other integrated gatherings. There was a lot of danger in this.

In one instance, National Wake's drummer Punka was detained the day before they were to play the Free People's Concert on Wits University grounds in Johannesburg, a neutral area where Black and white citizens could congregate. "It was a direct targeting of Punka by this cop who couldn't stand the fact that we were living free amongst all this bullshit," Kadey explains. The band would refer to this officer as "Bolina", eventually writing

26

an eponymous song about him. "We were playing on the Saturday or the Sunday, and Punka was busted on that Friday, which meant he went to jail through the weekend. You couldn't get anyone out until Monday. It screwed us because we couldn't play without our drummer."

This lit a fire under the band. To combat another potential arrest, National Wake forged an illegitimate company, stamping passbooks to indicate the bandmates were employed under DMZ, or démilitarized zone, Productions, so the Khoza brothers could travel safely to and from the band's communal house. Kadey explains, "We'd resisted playing the game on any level, but once it started getting rough, we decided that's what we'd do. It was like life during wartime. You just find ways to go between, to find your way through the minefield, which we managed to do for three years."

National Wake released just one album, in 1981, which sold approximately 700 copies before being forcibly shelved.[38] Their dissenting lyrics, rife with anti-apartheid sentiment, could now be heard loud and clear. "That brought down a lot of pressure from the police," Kadey says. The band had existed under heavy surveillance before the album's release; after, their house became subject to daily police raids, the album only fueling persecution from officers. "They would visit our commune three times a day, just come in and out with harassment. It took its toll."

Kadey compares life during apartheid to living in a pressure cooker, saying, "Ultimately, it wore us down." In 1982, National Wake would end, the four members going their separate ways. Lasting even three years was an impressive feat for a South African band like theirs. "The end was very depressing. It just fell apart," Kadey recalls. But National Wake was so much more to the guitarist than its bitter end. "The band became my way of being able to express my protest and fight my war."

Their disbandment would not be the end for National Wake. Fanzines and bootleg tapes echoed throughout the subsequent post-punk scene of the 1980s and '90s from which many bands, informed by a National Wake blueprint, would spring.[39] Into the final years of apartheid, officially ending in 1994, the South African underground would continue to nurture multi-racial bands and foster their unique fusion of punk rock, funk and reggae, with the hybridized ska-punk eventually becoming abundant. Ska-punk stalwarts Fuzigish, Leek and the Bouncing Uptones from nearby Pretoria, and Cape Town's Hog Hoggidy Hog became committed to merging the traditional sounds of their African upbringing – often introducing ghoema rhythms and kwela melodies that emerged from the jazz popularized in the townships – with the intensity of punk, perhaps another push against the legacy of segregation that had shadowed the nation for so long.

Years later, the band's influence would spread further beyond South Africa, thanks to documentaries like *Punk In Africa* (2012) and *This Is National Wake* (2022), and the compilation album *Walk In Africa 1979-1981* (2013). Before such projects reached the masses, some held the erroneous belief that protest music hadn't existed in apartheid-era South Africa. The burial of their music and the group's demise amidst the pressures of living under the regime meant Kadey himself believed National Wake had failed in their mission to spread a message of freedom, explaining to the *Guardian*, "We'd started with a vision that this was actually a way to move to something much brighter, a better South Africa. We dreamed that we were going to transcend all the bullshit and that people would hear our stuff and it would happen."[40] Failure could not be further from the truth.

While Gary and Punka Khoza would sadly pass away before they could witness National Wake's resurgence, their songs still touch people to this day. National Wake lives on; their music, their lyrics and their very existence standing as a testament to the power of music.

The 1970s birthed a musical and cultural revolution, the earliest examples of punk resounding with an urgency still felt today, with this era coming to – for many – define the genre. When it found a foothold among the youth of clashing Northern Ireland and warring South Africa, as part of this emerging global tapestry, punk was only amplified, that urgency morphing into severity, each angry lyric sounding far more grave, more prescient. Some focused their frustration on ostracization and loneliness while some sought normalcy, aspiring for a semblance of adolescence and an escape from their more sombre reality; others urged their peers to stand up in the face of brutality, to fight their aggressors and call for equality. Carving out hidden refuges, taking to the streets, protesting side by side, punks have stood, their music as their message, and stared their oppressors directly in the eye, their mere existence posing a threat.

This decade would only mark the beginning of punk's political ascent. Since inception, punk – forever multifaceted in its targets, its potential, and its fight – has been readied as a powerful weapon.

Chapter 2

1980s: Eager to Live at Any Cost

Growing geopolitical tensions and their global ripple effects became punk's new battleground as the 1980s marked a pivotal time in a years-long power struggle: the Cold War.

Lasting from around 1945 until the early 1990s, this marked a strained period for much of the world. Born from post-war competition, the democratic United States and the communist Soviet Union both contended for global sovereignty following World War II's devastation. The two world superpowers, and their respective allies – the U.S. with many Western European countries, and other nations that came to form the Western bloc; the Soviet Union allying with many Central and Eastern European countries, and other states across Asia and South America, to form the Eastern bloc – were entangled in a bitter rivalry.[41]

It was an intense time of capitalism versus communism, a power-hungry pissing contest on many levels – political, economic, ideological, even celestial. Dissension played out on the world stage through a series of proxy wars over the spread of communism in places like Korea and Vietnam, attempts to achieve military superiority through the stockpiling of nuclear arms, and efforts to assert dominance among the stars through the Space Race. The Cold War had far-reaching implications, and the rise of General Augusto Pinochet's dictatorship in Chile would be a byproduct of this struggle for supremacy.

In 1973, Pinochet came to power by way of a bloody military coup that overthrew democratically-elected President Salvador Allende. The U.S. government – partly weary of Allende's socialist policies and motivated by its own economic interests – played a controversial part in the takeover, providing a still-debated level of assistance to the Chilean forces that carried out the coup.[42] To counter communism's spread, the U.S. helped put Pinochet in power, and for nearly two decades, the Chilean people suffered for it. The general's authoritarian rule was widely characterized by repression, censorship, and human rights abuses. According to *NPR*, under his leadership, thousands were killed or forced to disappear, with 38,000 more taken as political prisoners, many of whom were tortured.[43]

Chilean-American author and second cousin of the overthrown president, Isabel Allende, remembered the coup in a 2013 interview with human rights organization Amnesty International. She recalled, "In 1973 and 1974 the atmosphere among the people I knew – students, journalists, intellectuals, artists, workers, etc – was very somber. We were scared."

Pinochet used fear as a powerful tool. "He controlled the military, the judiciary and there was no Congress; there was no freedom of the press, no habeas corpus, no right to dissent," Allende explained, asserting elsewhere, "It is very hard to live in fear. Out of necessity, one adapts rapidly."[44]

A decade after the coup, a band would emerge against this backdrop of terror, igniting a movement among Chilean youth and playing a crucial role in the dictator's eventual downfall. In 1984, four Santiago teens – Daniel Puente Encina, brothers Iván Vanchi Conejeros Vergara and Miguel Conejeros Vergara, and Francis Sebastián "Tan" Levine – became the Pinochet Boys, their very name a target on their backs.

"To name our anti-fascist band Pinochet Boys seemed, to us, to simply fit the times and circumstances we were living in," explains Puente Encina, the group's bassist, vocalist, and chief lyricist. With years living under

Pinochet's thumb, they saw themselves as his fed-up sons. "Pinochet was a kind of very severe father figure who told us what to do, how to dress, and even when to go to bed. We were his rebellious children."

The dictatorship marked a time of anxiety and general despondency for the Chilean people. "The coup, Allende's assassination, and the slaughter of thousands left a population sunk in depression," Puente Encina details. "We were so tired of that feeling, and the only genuine expression we had was to rebel."

However, as is becoming a common thread, many forms of artistic expression were deemed an affront to the dictatorship. Forming a band proved a near-impossible endeavor. "They closed universities, they closed cultural centers, many clubs," musicologist Javier Rodriguez Aedo told the *Guardian* of the Pinochet era.[45] Instruments were scarce, music venues virtually non-existent, not to mention the risks of speaking out against the regime. "On one side, many of these musicians didn't have enough to eat for many years, while others left [Chile] out of fear – scared that something could happen to them and they would be taken prisoner," Rodriguez Aedo added. Imprisonment, torture and death were ever-present threats to outward opposition. Protest music became a rarity.

Puente Encina remembers one of the first casualties of Pinochet's coup: Victor Jara. The renowned folk singer-songwriter, whose anthem "Venceremos", or "We Will Overcome", was used during Allende's presidential campaign, was arrested and detained at the National Stadium with thousands more. Jara was reportedly beaten, his fingers smashed, and then told to play guitar and perform for his fellow detainees. It is written that he defiantly responded to the brutality singing "Venceremos". Days after the coup, he was executed, for his communist beliefs, political activism and powerful words. In his posthumous "Manifesto", he shares a prophetic message, lilting in Spanish of "a man who will die singing, truthfully singing his song" – Jara received at least 23 gunshot wounds, his body carelessly dumped in public to be identified by passers-by.[46]

Even facing such dangers, the Pinochet Boys were determined to musically express themselves. "We were just really eager to live at any cost, even when it might result in our deaths." "¡Yo no tengo miedo!" they would chant in their "La Música del General"; young men who could have died singing, truthfully singing their song, proclaiming "I'm not scared!"

"We were hungry for culture in that repressive, dull system," Puente Encina explains of the music, looks and attitude entering the country with those returning from Europe and the States. "We felt, somehow, that we were allowed not only to identify with the stream of new artist ideas but also participate in it, to take a leading role even in such dark times as those we lived in. We played whatever we felt like playing. In terms of political positioning and attitude, though, we were punks, totally anarchist and libertarian, and by far the wildest and most controversial band in Chilean history." Controversial indeed, the group's very existence a brilliant flash – and therefore a marked threat – against the somber reality of Pinochet's reign.

Pinochet Boys started as members of a small artistic-subversive collective, which brought together writers, poets, and musicians rebelling against every facet of the system they were forced to live under.[47] "We were a community of weirdly dressed freaks existing within a cradle-to-grave conservative society," he says. "There was no life at all, even less so for young people."

The scene, made up of fellow political punks like Los Prisioneros (The Prisoners), Indice De Desempleo (Unemployment Rate), and Políticos Muertos (Dead Politicians), ran on participation and collaboration, occasionally coalescing with Santiago's metal scene.[48] Their events and performances were self-organized and produced on non-existent budgets. "It was our form of escape from the reality of the dictatorship. With these completely underground actions, we were free to set our own rules... Well, until cops came to put a stop to it, rough us up, and put the unluckiest of us in jail."

Pinochet Boys weren't initially a direct target of the

government until, one day, they were. Aside from their contentious moniker, their extreme performances tipped off authorities to the underground events. "We were a bunch of maniacs on drugs giving the final performance of our lives, each and every time." Puente Encina recalls one show where, during their song "Botellas contra el pavimento" ("Bottles Against the Asphalt"), he thought to smash a bottle on the stage for effect. The glass, however, didn't break. It ricocheted off the stage and into the audience, hitting a spectator. "Immediately, everybody started to throw bottles everywhere; it was complete madness. The venue ended up totally trashed, and we had to run from the police with our guitars and drums under our arms.

"Every concert ended up in chaos. We never were able to finish even one show: we were always stopped by the police."

Many of their gigs presented more dangers than flying bottles. On stage – the band brandishing a repertoire of treasonous songs – they were beaten, shot at, and, in one instance, nearly electrocuted when someone threw buckets of water onto their improvised stage. Puente Encina says these unpredictable moments were also liberating. "Playing in constant danger was in itself an act of courage and rebellion… We had nothing to lose. Death could be waiting just around the corner. The worst possible outcome would be to die of boredom."

Soon, military officials began surveilling the band, following them and at times apprehending them solely based on how they were dressed, or for wearing their hair shaved or colorful. "When the band gained some traction, we were warned that we were on the government's radar. We couldn't believe it at first." Still, the Pinochet Boys were steadfast. Their protest became paramount, itself an act of survival against their repression. "We weren't really aware of the sort of risks we were taking. Violence was normal at the time; you witnessed it everywhere. We grew up with it, and we were still so damn young."

The Pinochet Boys became the epicenter of an anarchist movement among the country's youth. Coupled with an uprising from Chile's impoverished urban community, the movement would eventually contribute to the outcome of the National Plebiscite of 1988, a revolutionary moment securing Pinochet's fall from power. A new constitution had been enacted in 1980, dictating a presidential referendum be held in 1988 to decide on another eight years of Pinochet rule. A near 56% of voters rejected extending the dictator's presidency[49] – fear would rule the people no longer. By spring 1990, Chile would transition to a democracy headed by Patricio Aylwin, who made it a mission during his time in office to document the human rights abuses buried by the Pinochet regime.

Before they could witness such a victory, however, the Pinochet Boys were forced from Chile when it became too dangerous. "They started really hunting us," he recalls, "with beatings and terrible threats, until we – the band – finally left the country."

During their time together, only two of the Pinochet Boys' songs were released on cassette, occasionally circulating underground radio programs. Yet, their messages – full of beautiful angst and infectious bravery – resounded, galvanizing the country's youth towards change. "Of course, in the '80s, we didn't realize what our music could mean or what impact it might have," explains Puente Encina. "What we did was what was most important to me, and that was to musically express what we felt." These songs live on in the annuls of Chilean history as a reminder of what just a few defiant voices can achieve in the face of oppression.

As with the Pinochet Boys, this decade would see another group of punks do the same, their amplified voices perhaps an impetus for the Cold War's impending thaw. Across the Atlantic Ocean, the Berlin Wall would be one of the most potent symbols of these tensions. Erected in Germany in 1961, the Wall stood as both a physical barrier and an emblem of the extreme ideological and political differences that had divided the globe for decades. Following Germany's defeat in the Second World War, the nation was divided into occupation zones, with the United States, Great Britain, France and the Soviet Union each taking control. The city of Berlin, while part of the newly Soviet-controlled territory, was also divided amongst countries.

As Cold War politics became more pronounced with time, a divided Germany in turn felt the strains. A partition – approximately 13 feet tall and 96 miles long, cast in concrete and fortified by barbed wire, watch-towers and a 'death strip' made up of anti-personnel mines and automatic firing devices – would bisect the capital, cutting off the East from the West. The German Democratic Republic (GDR) lived under strict Soviet rule, while the Federal Republic of Germany (FRG), existed under the control of American, British and French powers.[50]

Everyday life for the people of East Germany differed significantly from their Western counterparts. In the GDR, a one-party socialist state controlled many aspects of citizens' public and private lives, dictating everything from what could be consumed, be taught, and where citizens could travel, with movement to capitalist coun-tries requiring state approval, typically only permitted in rare, exceptional circumstances. On the other side of the Wall, the FRG, with its liberal democratic ideals, offered citizens more personal freedoms.

From 1972 onwards, the industry and agriculture in the GDR was government-owned, and its economy was centrally planned, leading to supply shortages of goods like food, medicine and fuel, little variation in consumer goods available, and lengthy queues to obtain basic essentials. Items as seemingly conventional as pots and pans, even thimbles, were in short supply[51] along with fruit, building materials and spare parts. The FRG had a market economy, with general prosperity and variety. Eastern citizens adhered to the strict hyper-political doctrine while a vibrant and diverse cultural scene flourished in the West. In a *Guardian* essay, English novelist and filmmaker Chris Petit described living in West Berlin in 1984, referring to his side as "less a city than an advertisement for a controlled kind of hedonism."[52]

In the GDR, by contrast, the Stasi, the state's secret police, closely monitored citizens, often with the help of spies and informants, to ensure compliance.[53] Political dissent was not tolerated. At the mere whisper of opposition, citizens could be surveilled and subjected to harassment or even arrest.

Decades into this division, people still pushed back against state-wide repression. For many youths in the 1980s, that forceful blow came in the form of punk. It gave them a booming voice through the monotone drone, a brilliant flash of defiance against the grey, and eventually a whetted tool to chip away at the Wall that symbolized their discontent. Acts like Leipzig's Wutanfall ("Tantrum") and East Berlin's Planlos ("Aimless") and Namenlos

41

("Nameless") began to emerge in East Germany, their music a middle finger to the authoritarian state that restrained them and its Stasi wanted to keep them in line.

"Life in East Germany for us was, on the one hand, characterized by the rigid structures of the dictatorship and, on the other hand, by the strong desire of our small group of punks to break out of these structures," remembers Jana Schloßer, Namenlos' lead singer.

Namenlos – comprised of Jana Schloßer and Michael Horschig – formed in 1983 when the GDR had a clear idea of how young people should look, think and act. Movements, like Free German Youth, or FDJ, were maintained to indoctrinate young citizens between the ages of 14 and 25 as productive members of the socialist society.[54] Therefore, many youth underground groups, be it punk, skinhead, or goth were considered "negative decadence" in East Germany, often perceived as threatening or superfluous and thus associated with capitalism and individualism, going against what was taught to the country's adolescents.[55] "Everything that did not correspond to these 'guidelines' was critically observed and persecuted by the state security," Jana recalls. "We were simply wired differently than the followers of the system. We wanted to find our very own way to live life as freely and happily as possible."

Punk soundtracked that endeavor, fueling their pursuit of freedom. Jana remembers, "The music expressed exactly the sense of life which I had at that time. I did not listen to the music like an 'art appreciation', but the punk music pierced me directly to the heart… The music had the same energy as me."

The band's provocative catalog, which included "DDR Staatsgrenze" ("GDR State Border"), "Lohnt Es Sich Zu Marschieren" ("Is It Worth Marching?"), and their most searing anti-fascist anthem, "Nazis Wieder in Ostberlin" ("Nazis Again in East Berlin"), detailed their collective experiences living in a conformist society under ever-present state repression. Their lyrics occasionally touched on relationships and work, but more often criticized the state institutions that restricted them, singing "Große Worte, zuviel Macht, haben doch nur Scheiße gebracht", or "Big words, too much power have only brought shit" amid chants declaring, "Nazi pigs in East Berlin."

"With the songs, we denounced the social injustices," Jana explains. "They were an attack on a rigid system, a fresh storm of words that wanted to swirl away the dust of the old structures."

By the time Namenlos were ready to play live, the state had labeled punks as undesirables, officially barring them from public spaces like bars, restaurants and youth clubs and restricting the acquisition of state-organized performance permits.[56][57]

That did not stop Namenlos. "We didn't even try to get such a permit. We didn't care. That was exactly what we rebelled against: that you needed a stamp for every shit and that the state ultimately wanted to decide what may be said or played – artistic freedom only if it fits into the ideological concept and bureaucratically regulated texts. The state representatives were not prepared for the straightforwardness and anger with which we shouted out our personal truth and our frustration about the social conditions."

Danger came with such dissent, and the Stasi attempted to wear people down. "The punks were detained and interrogated and kicked out of school and conscripted into the army," Tim Mohr, author of *Burning Down the Haus: Punk Rock, Revolution, and the Fall of the Berlin Wall,* described to Dazed. "They paid with their bodies to bring down the dictatorship."[58] Punks faced constant scrutiny and harassment for things as trivial as not looking like the photo on their official identification, and dodging recruitment by the Stasi as informants against their peers.[59] "Other risks included not being able to complete your education or having constant difficulties at work. Blackmail was also popular. The Stasi threatened to harm other family members or partners if you continued to be a punk or did not want to cooperate with the Stasi." Jana remembers one instance in which a fellow punk and friend was taken into the forest by the secret police with a bag over his head and was beaten.

This was likely Juergen "Chaos" Gutjahr, frontman of Wutanfall. In Mohr's *Burning Down the Haus*, he describes a situation in which the young punk had several run-ins with the Stasi, his bosses and two of his bandmates acting as informants to the secret police. By 1983, Chaos was summoned for police questioning several times a week. Authorities used physical violence, intimidation, demoralization, and, in one instance, interrogated him for 17 hours straight with no food or water. One afternoon, in the back of an unmarked police vehicle, he snapped, lashing out at the officers, telling one, "Shut your trap, you fucking pig." They placed a bag over his head and took him to the woods where he was beaten and kicked. Bleeding and battered, he was then taken to a station to sign a statement assuring he'd been treated well during his time in Stasi care.[60]

Namenlos also experienced the state's strong-arm tactics firsthand. The harsh, unjust reality only strengthened their resolve, even as the shadow of the Stasi, of jail, of manifold threats, loomed. "The pressure of the state created in us only more resistance... We had to be creative and look for niches in which we could be as we were."

Some churches in the East would play a vital role in the punk movement, becoming one of the few safe spaces for its adherents. Thanks to offene Jugendarbeit, or "open youth work", they indiscriminately opened their doors to youth, reaching out to those discriminated against, and those educationally or socially disadvantaged through programs and activities meant to prepare them for adulthood. This was different than movements like Free German Youth where oaths were taken, matching scarves worn, and memberships upheld. Less emphasis seemed to be on statewide conformity, more encouraging socialization and participation among the country's youth. Open youth work allowed punks the opportunity to meet, stage concerts, and record and circulate their music.[61]

Namenlos would play just three gigs before their arrest, all on church grounds. Their messages, now shouted to the masses, saw authorities react with further persecution. "They did not want to allow such 'radical critical voices' and were certainly afraid that this would become a thing. The head of the Stasi, Erich Mielke, had given his staff the instruction to no longer handle these elements with kid gloves and to strike hard." They began to crack down, with Namenlos mentioned by name in a Stasi training video, titled "War in Peace", according to Jana. Music, and those brave enough to create it, share it, shout it in the face of tyranny, were seen as a threat to be dealt with.

"Again and again, there were arrests," Jana continues. The Namenlos members were apprehended on the day they were scheduled to meet with each other to discuss what to do in the event of their arrest. "Maybe it was a coincidence, but it is more likely that the Stasi knew about our appointment."

They faced extensive interrogation, each given a punishment dependent on their cooperation level. Jana was sentenced to one and a half years in prison.

The punk revolution in the East continued even with Namenlos scattered and detained. The attitude and desire to see their repressive system crumble – it was all alive in the punks of the Republic. The punk underground in East Germany continued to foster a network of dissidence, breeding more young punks, many of whom were willing to pay the price to take control of their lives. By the end of the 1980s and the subsequent dissolution of the GDR, authorities pinpointed punk as the nation's top problem.[62] Despite attempts made to muffle their rebellious cries – following stints in jail, many punks would take to the streets again, ready to pick up their fight where they had left off[63] – it was a voice that only grew louder.

By the end of the decade, the Wall that dissected Germany would topple, making way for the country's reunification. While its fall in 1989 came from collective factors – the Peaceful Revolution movement's rise that called for East German liberation,[64] the continued weakening of governing powers as pressures for reform only mounted in the communist bloc[65] – punk would be one of the forces that incited its collapse. "A single blow rarely brings a wall or a system down," Jana explains. "Our work only joined the many smaller and larger hammer blows against the ideological structure of the authoritarian state."

Punks became a physical embodiment of rebellion in East Germany, something the government had so desperately tried to muzzle. Despite the attacks that bands like Wutanfall and Namenlos had to overcome, Jana remembers the great times they specifically shared as a band and the joy they were able to experience for the first time without restraint. She wonders, "Maybe it was exactly that which frightened the state."

As the years wore on, punk would continue its evolution, braving even more Cold War territory as it infiltrated Soviet Russia and gave life to Avtomaticheskye Udovletvoritely (Automatic Satisfiers) of St Petersburg (then-Leningrad), Moscow's avant-punk outfit DK, and Siberia's experimental psych-punk act Grazhdanskaya Oborona (Civil Defense). It would also find favor among China's youth, particularly following the 1989 Tiananmen Square protests, a series of student-led demonstrations that resulted in government crackdowns and the deaths of a still unconfirmed number of peaceful protestors – the estimate ranges from hundreds to thousands.[66] The oft-dubbed "Father of Chinese Rock", Cui Jian's "Nothing to My Name" had become an anthem among protesters in the weeks before the massacre[67] – its resolute lyrics proclaiming little to offer but love – and, afterward, fueled a punk movement among the nation's fed up youth.

As Jana said, it is rarely a single blow that brings a wall or system down; and while music alone cannot topple a regime, it is something to fear. The hope, the belief, the strength music inspires, the voices it emboldens, it's enough to strike panic within all oppressors.

Political pressures, activism and protest in all forms, together with music, have played their part in putting dissent on the historical record. In these instances, punk stood side by side with others, a honed tool to dismantle structures, frighten their oppressors and push for a freer world.

Chapter 3

1990s: Not Alone in the Darkness

The turn of the decade was ushering in a radical new world.

The Revolutions of 1989, one of which led to the dismantling of the Berlin Wall, would span the next few years, catalyzing a domino effect of movements worldwide and marking what would be known as the Fall of Communism. The Eastern Bloc would dissolve in a wave of pro-democracy moves across Central and Eastern Europe in countries like Poland, Hungary, Czechoslovakia and Bulgaria.[68] [69] Further independence movements would result in the collapse of the Soviet Union and establishment of 15 independent countries, including Armenia, Azerbaijan, Belarus, Kazakhstan, Moldova, Russia, Turkmenistan and Ukraine. It was against this backdrop that a post-Cold War Era was taking shape, the '90s welcoming an age of transition.

Concurrently, the Internet age was on the rise, seeing the globe grow increasingly interconnected as rapidly evolving technology, like the World Wide Web and the cell phone, shaped how we communicated and shared information, beginning to mold modern culture as a whole. Suddenly, there were new forms of interaction and expression,[70] the years giving way to innovation after innovation: Google, the Macintosh personal computer, the genesis of SMS messaging, the Nokia 1011. Connection surged, networks broadened, but unity didn't necessarily experience the same uptick. While the '90s are often remembered, by some, as a period of relative peace and prosperity as revolutions signaled change technologically, socially and globally, for many, that is far from reality.

As the decade unfolded, so too did worldwide discord. Punk found a foothold in Yugoslavia early on, spreading nationwide after it first reared its defiant, mohawked head in the 1970s. Evidence of the genre's fledgling influence in the region can still be seen graffitied on a stretch of asphalt in Rijeka, Croatia. "Paraf punk" the runny white paint-turned-cultural heritage site reads – once a relic of 1977, today, an enduring monument to one of the former nation's first punk bands.[71]

Unlike other Eastern European countries following WWII, the Socialist Federal Republic of Yugoslavia – a multi-ethnic federation of six distinct republics: Bosnia and Herzegovina, Croatia, Macedonia, Montenegro, Serbia, and Slovenia – remained neutral with the onset of the Cold War, aligning with neither warring power. Yugoslavia instead adhered to a socialist system built on brotherhood and unity. Citizens could travel unrestricted outside the country, indulge in foreign goods, and were exposed to many Western influences, like jazz and rock music, as well as trends depicted through Hollywood films.[72]

By the time a young Croatian, Dario Adamic – Adam – discovered punk in the early 1980s, Yugoslav bands like Slovenia's Panktri and the aforementioned Paraf had infiltrated the nation's consciousness. What records were released by state-run companies or what information could be gleaned from the pages of popular music magazines became a form of punk education for Adam, who today heads two labels – Goodwill Records and No Plan Records – dedicated to the genre. Local fanzines broadened the young punk's horizons, these pieced-together rags making tangible an entire scene near his coastal home city of Split.

"It opened a whole new world to me," he remembers. "There were bands from around the corner that I had no idea existed because they were not big, they were not in the mainstream media. I discovered something I was totally oblivious to."

Fanzines and various other culture publications like Serbia's *Džuboks*, Slovenia's *Mladina* and its literary journal *Problemi*, and Croatia's *Polet*, allowed punk culture to thrive in the late 1970s and 1980s. By giving young people room to be themselves and to feel seen, a movement was nurtured between their pages.

Just as it was for adolescents in countries where the genre was birthed, punk allowed the young people of Yugoslavia to express themselves and foster an identity separate from that of the socialist state. Unlike punk culture elsewhere, that of pre-war Yugoslavia was not necessarily an underground culture. It didn't have to be.

Youth culture was encouraged in Yugoslavia, with the state providing young people with numerous resources, funding publications like *Polet* and establishing student cultural centers. Founded following student-led protests in 1968 calling for social and economic reform to the socialist system, these centers gave young people invaluable physical spaces to share art and exchange ideas.[73] [74] Government programs licensed rock recordings, organized concerts, and, to an extent, gave homegrown bands the freedom to shout their pointed lyrics. That is not to say the scene existed without censorship – there were certain subjects deemed too taboo by the government to lyricize, like the socialist party's legitimacy, notions of nationalist separatism or critiques of then-longtime president Josip Broz Tito. Art often went through a committee before being made publicly available; music determined to conflict with the federation's socialist values was subject to a 31.5% "kitsch tax". To avoid this, acts began to self-censor or code their messaging: Paraf's "Narodna pjesma", or "National Song", with its anthemic cries of "There's no better police than our police" sounds like an impassioned paean to state authorities but is rather a song damning police repression that the scene faced.[75]

State-sponsored publications weren't safe from government scrutiny either. *Polet* was known to tout anti-government sentiments and, when asked by officials to refrain from publishing such articles, refused. The government began to spurn the publication.[76] When *Problemi* devoted three issues to the punk scene, the censorship committee criticized inclusion of anti-socialist lyrics and photographs sullying Titoist symbols.[77] Editors published the issues anyway with the censored content blacked out, shedding light on the state's suppression of free speech.[78]

Yugoslav punk, as it evolved, would become something unique, but also singular to the subculture as a whole. It became sonically and stylistically an amalgamation of many foreign and domestic influences – at first, pulling heavily from early British punk and then perfecting the post-punk style of the 1980s, all while infusing an Eastern European energy into the mix. The resulting sound was both quintessentially fast and loud while being musically robust and lyrically rich, a unique medley that would soundtrack the nation's final few years.

As the 1990s dawned, punk would change just as Yugoslavia did with the onset of war. The federation had, for years, been a breeding ground for religious and ethnic tensions between the groups that made up the patchwork nation, with historical animosities dating back to the early 20th century. Throughout Tito's decades-long rule, the dictator – his leadership viewed as both authoritarian and benevolent – promoted unity. Tito's united Yugoslavia would, however, not hold for very long in the wake of his death. High inflation and growing debt would mar the decade, with economic disparity between the republics leading to pushes for autonomy as no subsequent leader able to inspire harmony within the federation emerged. As these challenges persisted and ethnic divides grew, the decade saw a series of conflicts, commonly referred to as the Yugoslav Wars, result in the violent breakup of the federation, its republics eventually becoming independent countries.[79][80][81]

In a nation suddenly divided by war and insurrection, many of its punk adherents were caught in the crossfire.

"This was a generation of young people who really believed in transformation: of transforming their world, creating their own culture, doing things differently," Dr Vladislav Beronja, Assistant Professor of Slavic and Eurasian Studies at the University of Texas, explains.

"The rug was just swept beneath their feet, and their world – the world they thought they lived in, that they could transform – suddenly disappeared before their eyes, actually violently crumbled."

Prior to the violence, a rich, multicultural scene had been nurtured, but that could no longer exist. As Dr Beronja details: "Suddenly, they had to choose sides. Not only that, they suddenly saw their compatriots getting bombed, or their government sending tanks to the neighboring republics … It was really a dark time."

This federation-wide divide forced many cultural scenes to reckon with the schism, and the overarching rock scene would splinter. Some bands took up arms against the surfacing violence, with anti-war and anti-nationalist stances, where others who had long created politically-charged music before the fighting began to dissolve with the onset of war. On the other side, some touted nation-alistic views and championed their respective countries' fight for independence, where others were mobilized to the frontlines to fight. In the wake of this, cultural and musical scenes of the once-united federation lay rela-tively dormant.

"There were bigger fish to fry," Adam remembers. "There was a war in your country and maybe [music is] not anymore the first thing you think about when you wake up in the morning. When this madness all started, I would say that fewer bands were active."

Some groups in the region continued to make music motivated by Yugoslavia's sudden upheaval. Acts like Psihomodo Pop, a cult-favorite pop-punk outfit from Croatia, were among those who took a nationalistic stance at the start of the wars, releasing the morale-boosting "Hrvatska mora pobijediti" ("Croatia Must Win"). "Hrvatska, Hrvatska, Hrvatska, Hrvatska mora pobijediti," the chorus plays, followed by chants of "Za slobodu" ("For the freedom").

Psihomodo Pop frontman Davor Gobac said of the song, cited in the introduction to Svanibor Petton's *Music, Politics and War in Croatia in the 1990s*, "We recorded a true punk piece with which I hope to stimulate the blood of the guardsmen on the front lines to circulate faster... People are removed from normal life, buried in trenches, their houses are destroyed, and I have no motive at the moment to write a gentle love song..."[82]

Gobac, alongside members of other Croatian outfits like Film, Parni Valjak and Prljavo kazalište, would also join the cross-generational, multi-genre mega-group Hrvatski Band Aid. Together, they released the patriotic benefit single "Moja domovina" ("My Homeland") in 1991, during the initial days of the Croatian War of Independence. Singing "Moja domovina, moja domovina", artists proclaimed their country's strength and resilience, assuring listeners that "Cijeli svijet je sada sa nama" ("The whole world is now with us") and "Novi dan se budi kao sreća osvaja" ("A new day is awakening, conquers like happiness").[83]

It was against the backdrop of these early conflicts that another group joined forces in the name of peace. From three influential punk bands – Serbia's Ekatarina Velika, Električni Orgazam, and Partibrejkers – the anti-war supergroup Rimtutituki was born. The 8-person project vocalized the anti-war movement that broke out in the Serbian capital of Belgrade.

Mass demonstrations began in 1991 with the outbreaks of devastating sieges, like those in the Croatian cities of Vukovar and Dubrovnik. They saw thousands of people march in protest against Serbia's president at the time, Slobodan Milošević, and his regime that desired Serbian sovereignty even to the detriment of other ethnic groups. Milošević's regime would play a major role in the conflicts, carrying out wartime atrocities as he sought to conquer territory within the crumbling federation.[84] [85] [86]

"We wanted to oppose Slobodan Milošević, the Serbian government, army, and their war and hate propaganda," shares Električni Orgazam guitarist Srđan Gojković "Gile" on forming the supergroup. "We wanted to send a message to our friends and audiences in other Yugoslav republics that we are not supporting official Serbian politics at those times, that we are strongly against it."

When many media outlets were "pushing the mantra: 'war is the only way'", Rimtutituki spread their message of opposition with their only single, "Slušaj 'vamo!" ("Listen Here"), an anthem asking for "Mir! Mir, brate, mir!" or "Peace! Peace, brother, peace!" throughout.

At one anti-war protest in Belgrade, the band did not receive government permission to perform, so they shouted their words of resistance from the back of a truck as it circled the city streets. "We knew that we can't stop the war, but we wanted our voice to be heard."

Rimtutituki saw quiet opposition from the authorities. "Their tactic was to let us do what we do, so they can say they are democratic," Gile says. "They did not want to throw us in jail and make martyrs of us. They were fake democrats; they wanted to show to the world that they can tolerate opposite opinions." Rimtutituki was blocked from all forms of government-controlled media like television, radio, and print. Still, their cries for peace resounded through the streets of Belgrade.

"Those were very strange times," Gile recalls. "It looked like everybody was for war and destruction – at least if you watched TV and read papers controlled by the state. I guess what we did at the time was that we gave some hope to the people that had the same opinion as us. It might have been the minority, but I think it meant a lot to some, knowing that they are not alone in the darkness."

Amidst a mass exodus of people from the country, music became an increasingly honed munition with which some fought for hope and humanity at a time when both were difficult to find. Especially during the brutal siege of Sarajevo, a nearly four-year-long blockade of the capital city of Bosnia and Herzegovina; punks took up arms, wielding their music as a means of survival.

During the city's prolonged occupation by Serb forces from 1992 until 1996, an underground scene managed to create a haven amidst endless atrocity. There were near constant bombings, an average of 329 mortar shells quaking the city every day. Mass civilian targeting occurred, like the Markale market massacres, where citizens were attacked as they bought basic goods or waited in bread lines.[87] The genocide and ethnic cleansing of Bosnian Muslims resulted in the overall deaths of more than 11,000 people.[88] Many more hideous war crimes surrounded the scene's evolution, with one of its most active participants being Sikter, who would perform in underground venues to audiences who risked their lives to hear them play. To seek refuge at a venue, concert-goers had to first evade the streets' dangers, especially the infamous Sniper Alley, where shelling and rifle fire were almost guaranteed. People made their way through a hail of bullets and mortar shells for music.

"We were young and eager for life, which in the bloody grayness of besieged Sarajevo one received only in small spoonfuls," writes their former bassist-guitarist Nebojša Šerić Šoba in a 2022 personal essay.[89]

Sikter would play their first wartime gig in 1993 at the club Kamerni Teatar 55, the concert lasting "as long as the gasoline for the generator."[90] This was life under siege, civilians often without electricity or water, and limited access to food.

"The hunger for a normal life prevailed," he writes. "So many people were ready to risk their lives for two hours of any music whatsoever." As a soldier in the besieged city, the musician had to report to the frontline afterwards, a bitter reality that had momentarily been washed away by the crackle of shitty speakers and the fearless energy of the room.

Šoba describes an existence between two worlds – one under the spotlight, performing for an insatiable crowd; in the other, his military vehicle is suddenly struck, he's thrown to the ground by explosions, and forced to carry on to the frontline by foot.

He writes, "Dreams and real life were intertwining with the brutal reality of the place and time I found myself in. How had I gotten used to this type of life? Would this forever be my "normal"? Will I live to see the next concert?" Per his essay's title, this was "just another day" in Sarajevo.

Though a ceasefire agreement was reached in 1995 and an official end to the siege declared in February 1996, fighting would continue for several years as republics battled insurgencies and gained independence across the decade.[91]

In the years following the wars, the punk scene would become reinvigorated as homegrown acts reunited and new groups formed. At the time of writing, two-thirds of Rimtutituki are going strong, with Električni Orgazam and Partibrejkers still active. Their message perseveres.

Pre-war Yugoslav punk remains a testament to the unyielding belief of the youth of a once-united nation. It still resounds with their desire to rebel against conformity and transform the society around them. While punk may no longer be the dominant sound and subculture of the region today, perhaps it's like the asphalt in Rijeka, scarred with the "Paraf punk" graffiti – it is faded, but forever.

Words, like music, persevere too – they have power. "War is not my language" – the words printed across a T-shirt in English, Hebrew, and Arabic – flashes across the screen in Liz Nord's 2004 documentary, *Jericho's Echo: Punk Rock in the Holy Land*. Over B-roll, the members of Israeli hardcore punk band Nikmat Olalim discuss change and their hope for peace between Israel and Palestine, two states that have, for decades, existed under the constant threat of war.

Following young musicians navigating life during the Second Intifada – meaning "uprising" in Arabic, referring to the sustained periods of protest from Palestinians against Israeli occupation – the film depicts a young scene attempting to make sense of the world around them. Triggered by the dissolution of the peace process at the Camp David Summit in 2000 when negotiations between Israeli Prime Minister Ehud Barak and president of the Palestinian Authority, Yasser Arafat, broke down, the Al-Aqsa Intifada ignited when Israeli soldiers began firing on Palestinian demonstrators. In the first three weeks, there was a considerable show of aggression from the Israel Defense Forces (IDF), who attempted to quickly quell dissent, reportedly discharging over one million rounds of ammunition.[92] Generations' worth of disputes and violence escalated further with suicide bombings, rocket blasts and sniper attacks, costing more than 4,000 lives.[93] [94] Through interviews with Israeli punk bands and brief glimpses into their makeshift shows, *Jericho's Echo* tells the complex story of a generation's struggle amidst the intense cultural, political, and religious unrest that marked this uprising.

A decade before the film, a fledgling scene would find its footing against the events of the First Intifada, the bands at its helm paving a way for the nation's punks years later. The genre first infiltrated Israel in the late 1970s. Pioneering acts like rock singer Rami Fortis, electronic rockers Chromosome, alt musicians Jean Conflict, and new wave HaClique introduced the country to the dingy and industrial stylings of these manifold genres. The pure punk sound and attitude were far more difficult to find during this time, with bands like Cholera setting the precedent for the scene that would develop in the coming decades.

"Israel wasn't exactly a rock'n'roll country," Federico Gomez writes in hardcore punks Nekhei Na'atza's *From Nowhere Into Nothing: Recordings 1994-1997* liner notes. "Most people liked their music watered down and easy on the ears, and even information about mainstream bands and musicians from around the world was hard to come by."

At a young age, Gomez and his brother Santiago moved to Israel from Argentina. While living in a socialist kibbutz in Upper Galilee, having taken advantage of free international post available, they received their punk education. Sending correspondence to the United Kingdom, Japan and everywhere in between, they began reaching out to various fan clubs and magazines, eventually bands and record labels around the world, gaining tapes, zines, or pen pals in return.

"While our peers were busy thinking about their upcoming army service and where to score booze for next weekend's drinking binge, our main interest during the last years of high school was to somehow get involved in this DIY, worldwide hardcore-punk scene," Gomez writes. In late 1990, the siblings, alongside brothers, Oded and Yonni Tal, held their first rehearsal for what would become Nekhei Na'atza in a high school bomb shelter. Later joined by Etay Levi, they would supply the

Israeli punk scene with something that had been virtually absent: a distinctly political voice, particularly one with an anti-Zionist stance.

As Gomez submersed himself in the world of punk, the First Intifada broke out due to growing frustrations over Israel's military occupation and land expropriation, bringing his attention to the oppression of Palestinian people. Though difficult to find Palestinian punk bands active at the time, that doesn't mean they didn't exist or that their plight went unnoticed. The persecution Palestinians witnessed at the hands of the Israeli state would inform much of Nekhei Na'atza's music, their lyrics critiquing the very ideology upon which the nation was built. In 1994, they released an album titled תתכחשו ליהדות, or *Renounce Judaism*. The 7" featured growling, rage-filled tracks like דת גזענית ("Racist Religion"), לעבדות תמכרו את המתנחלים ("Sell the Settlers to Slavery"), and רצח עם שלם ("Entire Genocide"). The band believed that this outward opposition to the state was, as Gomez writes, "the direction a nascent Israeli punk scene should aim towards."

Palestinian oppression has been a major cause among the borderless scene. In 2002, Spanish punks Ska-P shared "Intifada", crying for the "liberación" of Palestinians, as Norwegian punks Honningbarna shout "Fri Palestina" in 2011's track of the same name. English bands like Oi! punk pioneers Angelic Upstarts and '90s street punks The Restarts crafted songs 2015's "Until Palestine Is Free" and 2019's "Uprising" respectively – calling out the lives and homes lost, the people displaced and rights stripped, with the latter anthem sneering, "It's time to rise up open your eyes."

With this oppression on their own borders, at the hands of their state, the Israeli punk scene that evolved proved both close-knit and divided. In *Rock in a Hard Place: Music and Mayhem in the Middle East*, author Orlando Crowcroft explains that within the small but passionate underground existed a subsect referred to as "arso punk". He writes ars is Hebrew slang, meaning "bully" or "hooligan". The term distinguished chaotic, thrashing, and often violent arso punks from its more politically conscious adherents like Nekhei Na'atza and melodic skate punks Haifa-formed Useless ID.[95]

The division extended beyond labels, with bands existing on a political and ideological spectrum. Nekhei Na'atza and their radical anti-state position occupied one end, with right-wing voices on the other. A similar dynamic features in *Jericho's Echo*, wherein, groups like Nikmat Olalim decry Israel's occupation of Palestine and militarization in their music and outreach, while others hold outlooks somewhere in the middle, using music as a means to evade hostilities – Useless ID, noted Nord in a 2005 interview with *FRONTLINE/World*, "play poppy love songs, not anti-occupation rants, because their lives are already mired in politics. Their music is a deliberate escape from that"[96] – continuing to the other end, where bands like Retribution embrace right-wing, nationalistic stances, sharing devotion to the state, and their military service.

The military – to serve or not to serve – was another contentious point. Israeli citizens, at 18, must fulfill mandatory time in the IDF, ranging from administrative work to full-fledged combat. Consequences for opting out included jail sentences. Even today, those who refuse to enlist risk being sentenced to repeated prison stints until they comply. Longer-lasting implications include being met with disapproval from family and society, potentially affecting job prospects, ability to obtain loans and more through adulthood. In the end, several bands never withstood the draft.

Some divided time between their respective bands and life on base. To Nekhei Na'atza's Etay Levi, punk was a lifeline during service. "Truth be told, I was annoyed by the army after the first five minutes and couldn't wait for them to kick me out," he adds in the liner notes of *From Nowhere Into Nothing*. "Unfortunately, they did not, but being able to be so close and head down to the bomb shelter to make some noise with my good friends whenever we wanted was life-changing."

In late 1994, Useless ID formed during founding guitarist Guy Carmel's stint as an army electrician.

"We were just a bunch of kids trying to live a relatively modern life in the Middle East influenced by Western culture," Carmel shares. "Then all of a sudden, you get dressed in uniform, they give you a gun, and you need to learn how to fight now." Some of Useless ID – like vocalist and bassist Yotam Ben Horin and lead guitarist Ishay Berger – dodged the draft.

Having moved to Israel from Brooklyn, New York, in his adolescence, Ben Horin, from the beginning, wasn't keen on his impending service. "That frightened me from the moment we moved there," he says. "My whole upbringing was American; my whole culture was different. Suddenly, I was in Israel, and in three years, I'd have to be in the army." It was while in high school that Ben Horin met Useless ID. With aspirations of touring the world, the band became a chance at escape for the young bassist, and he wasn't willing to give that up. "Once I knew that I wanted to do that, I was like, I'm gonna do anything I can to get out of this mandatory army service. It wasn't easy." Of his decision, he adds, "I didn't want to be restrained by anything. I wanted to be free."

Freedom to express their truth is clear in *Jericho's Echo*, depicting a scene as close-knit, described as a "small family", while remaining just as divided by personal views toward religion, politics, and by what being punk and Jewish meant to this new generation. "Many of the bands feel a responsibility to voice their discontent on everything from the Israeli occupation [of Palestine] to the religious right," Nord offered *FRONTLINE/World*.[97] Despite their differences, these punks shared a similar struggle as they fought for freedom in a place that predestined so much for them, their music an escape from politics and war, an act of rebellion against their environment. "They want to make music despite events around them and the pressure to follow a mainstream path. No matter where they fall in the ideological spectrum, they all share one belief: punk rock is freedom."

It is a freedom of expression seen globally, something that manifested in many different forms during this era. The '90s gave rise to the glossy, angst-ridden trappings of pop punk, but the decade also saw the ascent of the riot grrrl movement, which placed a ferocious feminism at the forefront, and welcomed the emergence of several Latino and Chicano hardcore groups, like New York City's Huasipungo, Chicago's Los Crudos and Youth Against, and Los Angeles' Tragátelo, in the wake of various political decisions – California's Proposition 187 that barred illegal immigrants from receiving health care and public education, the controversial North American Free Trade Agreement that hindered Mexico's indigenous population and the subsequent Zapatista uprising in response[98] – that greatly impacted their communities[99]

It is a freedom that refuses to be forced into compliance; a freedom that has given power to speaking up, to yelling lyrics that resound with truth; a freedom to share the stories of those without a voice and shout their protest across borders.

As the world continued to grow more interconnected, many of these punk's powerful words began to resound far and wide: state aggression is not my language. Censorship is not my language. Torture is not my language. Death is not my language. War is not my language.

Chapter 4
2000s and 2010s: Keeping the Flame Alive

The new millennium was a time of continued transformation. As the 2000s brought promises of a rapidly evolving digital age – increased global communication, accessibility to information and the widespread sharing of knowledge and ideas – it rested against complex political backdrops.

The global economy was in flux, taking a nosedive in 2007 when interest rates rose, debt bubbles burst and the housing market collapsed in a financial crisis known as the Great Recession.[100] The planet was becoming dramatically altered by the effects of climate change and global warming, with efforts toward renewable energy, sustainability and conservation growing increasingly dire with each diminishing ice cap. Commentary surrounding environmentalism began to take root in more bands during this time, one of the most outspoken being Chicago-formed Rise Against – 2006's "Ready to Fall" music video features harrowing scenes of pollution, deforestation, mining and oil drilling, wreaking havoc on the planet.

Terrorism was brought to the forefront at the turn of the century in the West. 2001's September 11 attacks saw 19 al-Qaeda-associated militants hijack four airplanes, piloting two into New York City's World Trade Center and one into the Pentagon in Washington D.C., resulting in almost 3,000 deaths, and the launch of a military campaign, known as the global war on terror. London subsequently saw the 7/7 bombings in 2005, causing the death of over 50 and injuring over 700 more, as one of countless global terrorist attacks in this new era.[101] American punks made music that either directly took aim at President George W. Bush and his war-mongering administration like '80s punk icons NOFX with their 2003 release *The War on Errorism* – the album's cover depicts a caricature of the U.S. leader painted in clown makeup – or took inspiration from the wars that resulted, such as those in Afghanistan and Iraq, like the West Coast hardcore titans Bad Religion did with their 2004 release, *The Empire Strikes First*. Green Day's pointed *American Idiot* from the same year saw political rebellion in the mainstream.

Like the rest of the world, punk, too, would undergo a major transformation. Adopting new doctrines to address these fresh grievances, it also navigated an increasingly unfamiliar terrain of 1s and 0s. As digital advancements only loomed, eventually welcoming greater accessibility via smartphones, punks could bring the underground to our fingertips. Suddenly, issues that plagued a once-distant scene now affected a global one, and faraway movements that once took time to come to light could be witnessed in real time, across borders. In 2007, one revolution would spark another when a teenager took to the streets of Yangon, the largest city in Myanmar, formerly known as Burma. The young, soon-to-be pioneering punk frontman, Kyaw Kyaw, joined tens of thousands of protesters against the country's ruling military junta, the curiously named State Peace and Development Council, in the anti-government demonstration, the Saffron Revolution.

The non-violent protests, which took place across the Southeast Asian country from August to October 2007, were spurred by a sudden spike in fuel prices following the government's removal of subsidies without warning. The price of oil rose by 66%, with the cost of natural gas increasing times five,[102] disrupting businesses that relied on generators and making public transportation unaffordable if not halting it altogether. This also caused prices of all other goods to skyrocket, a hefty blow to the people of the already-impoverished nation.[103] [104]

Mass protests erupted nationwide, thousands beyond Yangon in cities like Yenangyaung and Bago, and towns like Mogok, Chauk and Taungdwingyi, voicing their frustrations.[105] At the heart of the demonstrations was a desire to end the country's corrupt military rule, one characterized by decades of systematic repression, abuse and economic mismanagement often due to negligent military spending. They wanted democracy.[106]

A junta had been governing Myanmar since 1962, following General Ne Win's military coup that overthrew the Anti-Fascist People's Freedom League, which had been headed by democratically elected Prime Minister U Nu since the country's independence from British rule in 1948. Within the first weeks of military dictatorship, basic freedoms – press, movement – were being stripped, political parties done away with, and public gatherings limited or banned.[107]

The economy quickly deteriorated under this leadership, corruption becoming evident through the years – even after the National League for Democracy's resounding victory during 1990's multi-party elections, the junta refused defeat, holding tight to power and placing NLD's leader Aung San Suu Kyi under house arrest.[108] However, when the Saffron Revolution arose so too did hope for a better future, further blossoming when teams of Buddhist monks, whose red garments gave the uprising its name, took helm of the peaceful demonstrations.

Kyaw Kyaw remembers being amazed at the masses pouring into city streets, carrying signs and calling for change. According to the Global Nonviolent Action Database, it would have been uncommon for monks to take part in political matters,[109] but their involvement – at first, refusing alms or tithes from military officials and therefore refusing them Buddha's blessing, and then, leading the charge – held great significance.

"We think we will win this fight," Kyaw Kyaw remembers, feeling optimistic at the onset of revolution. He recalls assuming the military officials in the devoutly Buddhist country would have been respectful of the protests that saw monks on the frontline. "But we were wrong."

Authorities took violent action, clubbing and tear-gassing protestors, and firing into the crowds who had peacefully marched on Yangon. "After four or five days, they shot at the monks and demonstrators. A lot of people died," recalls Kyaw Kyaw. Since the protests began that August, the country's independent media organization Democratic Voice of Burma had been capturing the events, committing to tape acts of suppression from authorities. Protesters were filmed being carried off in vans or arrested out of suspicion during the demonstration's initial days.[110] The violence that came that September, though, met international eyes when civilians with cellphones and portable cameras captured and shared footage from the ground.

Eye-opening events that would have once been at the mercy of news cycles or word-of-mouth were now being broadcast for the world to see, brutal realities suddenly accessible from our back pockets. Due to the chokehold on information allowed in and out of the country during this time – internet access and mobile phone networks were temporarily suspended shortly after the outbreak of the incident[111] – the number of deaths is assumed to be much higher than the initially reported 31 casualties.[112]

"I was shocked," Kyaw Kyaw says, recalling feeling scared and angry at the same time. "People were crying and suffering… I'd never seen this before."

It was from the Saffron Revolution that he – having witnessed the military's devastation and smaller acts of peaceful resistance that continued in its wake – decided to start The Rebel Riot. This punk outfit would ignite a revolution all of its own.

Armed with a sound that has grown into a heavy, high-energy mix of their punk and hardcore influences, the fierce formula cuts listeners to their depths. "We sing what we see," Kyaw Kyaw explains. They critique aspects of their daily lives, shedding a light on widespread poverty and hunger in "Lower Class", laying bare human exploitation for profit in "Punk Against Sweatshops", pulling back the curtain on the country's opium and heroin epidemic[113] in "Drug Victim", and revealing the realities of "Street Punx" who "don't care for their fucking rules / We are still fighting for a way of life."

And fight they do, using their music as both a weapon and a wake-up call. "Fuck Religious Rules/Wars" unpacks the religious conflict between Buddhist and Muslim sects that has afflicted the nation for decades, singing how hate only breeds more hate. In "Stop All Fucking Wars", they ask on behalf of refugees, innocent people, and "children who are between the bomb explosions" that all wars be stopped. They scream about genocide and terror, noting from first-hand experience the horrors that come with conflict.

The Rebel Riot's messages feel universal. They approach songs with compassion while expressing the need for unity and support. In "United Forever Fight Together" and "Resistance", listeners are urged to be fearless in the face of tyranny, called to band together and rebel against injustice, declaring, "Smash the racists, change the system of the world." Kyaw Kyaw says, "Most people say our music is one they listen to feel more brave."

The band began playing to the small punk and alternative community within Myanmar. Now, after nearly two decades, The Rebel Riot has expanded beyond and, in many ways, become a movement.

"Lots of people from outside, they support, not just our music, they also support what we stand for, what we are doing," Kyaw Kyaw says of their mission. For them, it is one thing to speak out about what is happening around them; it is another to take action. The Rebel Riot has long been involved with several volunteer organizations, working tirelessly to serve their community, raising money and spending time on the ground. In 2013, they started a Food Not Bombs chapter in Yangon. The global, volunteer-led grassroots organization shares meals with the hungry in protest against war and poverty. For hunger to persist in the midst of abundance, the organization believes, is a complete skewing of governmental priorities.[114] Still, Rebel Riot take to the streets weekly, preparing and handing out rice or noodle-based meals to the city's poor and homeless population, sometimes giving food to more than 600 people in a single Saturday evening.

"Obviously, fuck the system, fuck the rich people, fuck the greedy," says Kyaw Kyaw. "You can complain, or whatever you want, after you read the newspaper… You can say, 'This is no good.' But how about me? What should I do? We are right here now, so we should start step-by-step for small change."

Even the smallest alteration can have a huge impact. "Revolution is not only changing outside; revolution is also changing yourself," the frontman says. "This is our philosophy for our life."

That philosophy bleeds into what The Rebel Riot seek to accomplish, with Kyaw Kyaw explaining, "We want to share our ideas with the young people. They create their own community with their own philosophy to do something." From there, he hopes a chain reaction will occur, that one revolution will spark another. "The idea is the revolution," he says. "After we die, the movement, the idea, it never dies."

After nearly a decade of work restoring democracy in the country, in 2021, Myanmar again found itself under the control of a military junta. The current leadership has taken action to smother the sounds of resistance, banning many outlets of free press, blocking access to several social platforms, and periodically blacking out internet access.[115] Still, The Rebel Riot and their revolution persists.

In May 2024, three years after the most recent military coup, the band released the album *To… Dear Comrade*, which features "Spring Nightmare", a gripping instrumental riddled with the sounds of banging pots and pans, rallying cries, gun fire and screams of terror soundtracking the resistant movement that broke out following the takeover. "This album is more than just a collection of songs," the band explain on Bandcamp.[116] "It's our traumas, anger, and energy, all mixed up with sadness. With these songs, we want to invite friends from all over the world to pay attention to what's happening in Myanmar and show solidarity."

"The whole country is in a shitty situation," Kyaw Kyaw shares with me, "so people are losing their hope."

Because of the current political landscape, he explains, it's easier for citizens to blame, hate, and fight one another rather than push against the military government. He says this is the time for people to support and care for each other.

"We share the positive, and we create hope in this community." With these words and with the swift flick of his thumb, a small flame dances from Kyaw Kyaw's lighter, illuminating the right half of his face. "Just create your own light, and around you is light."

Elsewhere, in the magenta glow of another light, frantic riffs and pensive notes are traded back and forth like the intrinsic tossing of a restless sea. From the melody comes a story, a true tale depicted in hushed vocals about a Syrian man who traveled from Turkey to Greece, swimming a six-kilometer expanse of the Aegean Sea one night with little but the moon lighting the way toward "oblivion or hope – I cannot tell."

"This song is for him and for all the other refugees," says Rashwan Zaza, the frontman of Dubai-based Ras Al Ghul, introducing "Catching Stars (Refugee Song)" on stage.[117] The song is personal for Zaza, who left his home in Damascus early in the 2011 Syrian Civil War. The ongoing conflict between the Syrian government and anti-government rebel groups has since displaced more than 14 million people, creating the world's largest refugee crisis to date.

Before the war, in the Syrian capital of Damascus, Zaza had formed the pioneering punk band Mazhott in 2008. "I was technically the only punk I knew in Syria," Zaza explains, detailing the country's small but zealous underground heavy metal scene, which included The Hourglass from Homs, Aleppo's progressive metal outfit Nu.Clear.Dawn and Latakia's death metal group Slumpark Correctional. Metal flourished at the turn of the century as the internet opened up the isolated nation and pirated music, often coming from Russia, exposed their youth to a world of sounds. The scene eventually became an umbrella outlet, so Zaza and the other members of Mazhott – drummer Dani Shukri, bassist Kareem Kouzbari, and guitarist Akram Darkashli – delivered their punk messages alongside the dense, distorted drone of their metal counterparts.

"I had kind of a social agenda in my head," he says. To bring about change, he felt it would be easier to reach more people through punk, writing all of their songs in Arabic. "If you want people to listen to what you have to say, you have to speak to them in their own language."

There was a political tinge to many aspects of Syrian life, but in the 2000s, there came – however short-lived – a kind of freedom of expression, as well. "That's what led to more people trying to do something different because being different in Syria was not a good thing. However, in that time, it was okay to express yourself creatively through music or writing or whatever." And it was the politics of Syria that, in many ways, informed such creation, he says. "That dictated, or at least gave a hint, like a flavor, to everything we did. You want change; you want something to be better, you know."

The band's 2013 EP *M for Mazhott,* which was recorded sporadically in the years leading up to the war and Mazhott's eventual disbandment, dissected and scrutinized their society. The live recording "Sai'een", reverberating with an undeniable angst, paints a desperate portrait of longing, trying to get by in a world where profit – money, success – is king. "It's just like how we live on the street, and nobody gives a shit about us," Zaza describes. "Bakaloria" is similar in its finality, chronicling the weight of the last year of high school in Syria's education system. "It kind of defines the rest of your life." Against a thrashed rendition of the traditional Syrian wedding song, they detail the realities of child marriage in "Awiha", a track portraying a 15-year-old girl's wedding day. They prod at the world around them, attempting to understand what it is to be young, what it means to look to the future, and what happens when you no longer have one.

Even with the aforementioned freedom to create such songs, the underground metal scene and its adherents still faced their share of persecution. "Metalheads have a certain look – long hair, black, piercings, stuff like that,"

Zaza explains. "That was very, very abnormal in Syria. So your parents didn't like it; the police didn't like it; nobody around liked it."

The scene was often subject to public scrutiny, metal often seen as synonymous with Satanism,[118] and government suspicion, which led to the underground being targeted and risking arrest. Even being a metalhead by proxy, like the members of Mazhott, didn't spare followers from the ebbs and flows of hostility from authorities. "The police would kind of go after the metalheads and anybody who kind of resembled a metalhead," Zaza says, comparing the crackdowns on the scene to full-blown hunts and the country's secret police to the Stasi in Germany.

"I got arrested for a week. And if you're arrested in Syria, that's a very bad experience that you might not come out of … You will just be like taken away, and you will be put in a dungeon somewhere where there's a lot of torture." Though his parents paid large sums of money to corrupt officers at the time of his arrest, easing some of the brutality of his week-long sentence, Zaza was still subjected to violence "just because I played some music."

When the Arab Spring, a wave of anti-government, pro-democracy uprisings that challenged widespread authoritarian rule in the region, began to crest over parts of the Middle East and North Africa at the start of the 2010s, there was a promise of revolution. After relatively successful protests, such as Tunisia's Jasmine Revolution and Egypt's January 25 Revolution, in which demonstrations ultimately overwhelmed authorities, led to the toppling of some long-standing regimes and resulted in social and political improvements in the nations, a collective optimism for change spread across the region.

Large-scale peaceful demonstrations erupted in Syria in March 2011 as citizens voiced their discontent with the country's leader, President Bashar al-Assad – his position heading the long-ruling Ba'ath Party had been passed down from his father following his death in 2000; his rule largely upheld the same authoritarian tactics. Citizens called for greater freedoms and for corruption to cease, with a key demand being the repeal the country's decades-old state of emergency.[119] The legal degree from 1962 allowed freedom and rights violations through surveillance, monitoring of printed and broadcast materials, seizure of property, and various restrictions placed on movement, residence, expression and more.[120] While Assad bent to some demands, announcing he would lift the emergency law and abolish the Supreme State Security Court, which worked to suppress state opposition,[121] it wouldn't be long before violence escalated, the government responding to protests with lethal force.

Unarmed demonstrators were fired at, and troops and tanks were deployed into cities to stamp out dissention. Neighborhoods identified as protest hubs could be encircled by heavy artillery and attack helicopters, and residents cut off from utilities, food, medicine and means of communication. During the uprising's first month, a reported 277 civilians were killed and 1,437 more arrested. Early days gave rise to various rebel and militant groups, such as the Free Syrian Army, and welcomed outside powers and foreign militias. What began as peaceful protests grew into an armed insurgency that, by the summer of 2012, had been given civil war classification.

Zaza was already on his way out, leaving Syria for Dubai months after the conflict began. It was a departure that had been planned beforehand, however, the uprising made returning impossible. Mazhott's other members would also go their separate ways, dispersing to neighboring countries or North America. The outbreak of war weighed heavily on the musician, burdening him with guilt.

"I was feeling really bad all the time. I was following the news all day long and all that crap. I felt like, 'Ah, fuck. I kind of skipped town and, you know, just escaped all this chaos. I should have been there with the people who were revolting against the dictatorship and all that.'" He continues, "After three years of really being completely consumed by that, I kind of had to take a step back and start to live life, in a sense."

Zaza would continue to make music in the United Arab Emirates, forming two bands, including Ras Al Ghul, and channeling those feelings into his art. Many songs he has written since leaving are related to the unrest in his home country, like "Catching Stars (Refugee Song)" about those who have been forced to rebuild their lives – some of them in a place far away, others from the rubble.

Since the onset of war, millions of Syrians have been displaced, forced to seek asylum across the region, in countries like Turkey, Lebanon and Jordan, and throughout Europe. According to the United Nations Refugee Agency, more than 70 percent of the country's refugees live in poverty. Access to basic services and opportunities for education and employment are limited and hopes of returning home have diminished as the war continues.[122]

"A lot of people I know, they don't have any place to go back to," he says. "If they go back to Syria, their homes are destroyed, not just their homes, their entire neighborhood."

Zaza details how his songs – many still to be released – became a way for him to come to terms with what was happening in Syria. "Every song that I've written has a big meaning to me," he says. "I feel them whenever I sing them." The tracks touch on friends back home, dealing with the unknown, or the feeling of being stuck. Some call for action, while others call out the paradox of fighting for peace. When they are released, perhaps they will offer a lifeline to those treading water in the night in search of home.

Art – in all its forms – has been a very human tool in revealing the realities of war, capturing the chaos and tallying the costs. War can take shape in a painting – as a mayhem of hues, a furor of forms – or on the page, blunt syllables stringing together ugly truths; it can appear in a song, chords gnashing at an assailing beat. War can also be portrayed in the form of a pig.

Flanked by masked figures with guns and crowned in a red beret, this particular pig looks menacingly from his seat – bubblegum-pink flesh wrinkled in a snarl, cloudy blue eye unblinking. He adorns badges and medals. U.S. dollars peek from his breast pocket. Microphones are pointed toward his gaping muzzle, eager to broadcast his squeals. Before him, shotgun shells and handguns litter a table already cluttered with bruised bananas, dismembered dolls, and plastic snakes mid-slither. A grinning skull and a glossy bust of a politician stare blankly from their positions amidst the chaos.

This is modern-day Venezuela, depicted brazenly by artist and photographer Nelson Garrido for *Ministro: ¿Cuál es su trabajo? – un extraño tributo al punk venezolano* (*Minister: What Is Your Job? – A Strange Tribute to Venezuelan Punk*), a 2019 album by Caracas-based Agente Extraño. This controversial image, a printed insert for the record, portrays a corrupt politician, pointing an accusing finger at the country's leadership.

"The print worker who was printing these materials

was detained and taken," shares Ernesto "Cuerdas Duras" Rojas, bassist-vocalist of Agente Extraño, recalling José Guillermo Mendoza's arrest. Ahead of the album's release, Mendoza was caught delivering a thousand inserts to the human rights organization, Provea, that had commissioned the album. He was stopped at a routine checkpoint by officers who inspected the materials. Deeming the image subversive, they apprehended Mendoza and took him to El Helicoide, an imposing building designed as the world's first drive-through mall but is now a detention center in the country's capital. [123]

"We thought they would be coming for us next," Rojas remembers.

Word of Mendoza's arrest got back to Provea and soon garnered the attention of citizens, artists, and activists who took to social media in protest. They hashtagged their criticism and cries for justice: #LiberenAJoseMendoza. He was released the next day.

The hashtag, showcasing the power of demands for Mendoza's freedom, can still be found across platforms. The very image that resulted in the print worker's arrest is present, the cloudy blue eye staring back through a phone screen, as people decry "cultural promotion and freedom of expression are not a crime".[124]

Ministro:¿Cuál es su trabajo? would be released as planned just days later, paying homage to Venezuela's once-passionate punk scene, which arose in the South

American country in the 1980s when the economy was crumbling, leadership was fluctuating, and political crises were playing out. However, the scene would soon be muffled by promises of change and a brief taste of prosperity that coincided with the beginning of Hugo Chavez's presidency in 1999.

Agente Extraño's tribute release pulled from a decades-old songbook that – in the 1980s and '90s – was rife with anthems flaying open the nation's tumultuous political landscape where power and human rights were frequently abused. They covered homegrown acts like Sentimiento Muerto (Dead Feeling) whose "Miraflores" pointedly asks, "Minister, what is your job?", wondering if it's the government's priority to drink and scheme, and Víctimas de la Democracia (Victims of Democracy) with "La Peste" ("The Plague"), equating the reality they were living to a plague that saw "bodies eaten by the bullets of order".[125] The album sounds just as current as the history it retraces.

Today, Venezuela faces an urgent humanitarian crisis, with this period of unrest beginning following Chavez's death in 2013, when the presidency changed hands to the former leader's second-in-command, Nicolás Maduro.

Not long after Maduro's ascension, the price of oil, a commodity upon which Venezuela relies for income, plummeted around the globe.[126] Recession ensued, inflation growing at devastating rates – it peaked at a staggering 63,000% in 2018[127] – seeing food, essentials like milk and flour, medicines, even staples like toilet paper, in increasingly short supply, and looting and violence spreading. Public unrest brewed as the economy collapsed and Maduro's mismanagement became apparent. Protests would erupt over citizens' discontent in 2014, but were quickly met with violence from security forces, resulting in a massive exodus of Venezuelans from their homes.[128] Nearly eight million Venezuelans have been displaced, the majority residing elsewhere in South America and across the Caribbean.[129]

The country's punk scene that was born from such strife decades prior failed to see a full-fledged revival. Rojas explains there was an initial blackout of protest songs when Chavez came to power and very few bands released music in the early 2000s, but the renewed unrest triggered bands to put together compilation albums, many of which Agente Extraño were a part of. Still today, Agente Extraño have devoted themselves to keeping punk alive for future generations.

When the band formed in 1997, they were writing songs about society, police brutality, homelessness, and other problems within their country. As the political landscape continued to evolve, the country's challenges followed suit. Agente Extraño's messages, too, turned more radical. "We began focusing our lyrics on what was experienced on the street… Our lives changed with the country, and our focus started turning from post-punk to a type of punk that we named 'Combat Rock'."

They have since amassed an equally poignant catalog as those of their pioneering predecessors, post-punk visionaries Sentimiento Muerto and hardcore exemplars like Deskarriados and Víctimas de la Democracia. "Mentiras" ("Lies") calls out Maduro and his false promises and "Darien" addresses the diaspora of over seven million Venezuelans since the beginning of the crisis. While newer track "Limbo Mental" lays bare the risks – imprisonment, even death – that come with speaking out, the horrors happening around them only fueled their need to cry out. The band began to pull inspiration from such horrors in "Inanicion" ("Starvation"), sparked following the deaths of two elderly brothers, who starved in their apartment after 72 hours without food in the Caracas' Puente de Hierro neighborhood.

"In the song 'Mi Amor', we talk about the strength of love in spite of adversities," he explains how songs can be more than ammunition, but a means of connection amid unrest. "It talks about how our love and strength to be with our loved ones is stronger than a thousand dictators, and that gives us the strength to keep on."

Their 2023 album, *Vivir Callados No es Vivir* (*Living Silenced Is Not Living*) speaks to this need for strength. Looking back on everything that's happened over the decades, Venezuela is examined under a harsh but very real light. "The album is raw, supercharged with reality," Rojas details. "It is our contribution to understand the present, compare it to the past, and try and fight and comprehend what we have to change so that there is hope for the future."

The title alone holds the key: living silenced is *not* living. Just as those who protested Mendoza's arrest refused to remain silent, perhaps Agente Extraño's *Vivir Callados No es Vivir* will inspire the same kind of action. "With the people that are currently in power, there is no hope for the future… They have taken everything away from us, and we must not let them take away our freedom to say what is wrong and to generate the strength needed to enact urgent change."

Much like its country, Agente Extraño has dramatically transformed since the '90s, yet, their music, and messages have endured. "I was left alone at the helm of Agente Extraño with other musicians that came and went because of the diaspora situation that the country was and is going through," Rojas explains. Their original drummer Sacha Torres and guitarist Ricardo "El Perro" Bermúdez left the country in search of a better life, with Bermúdez leaving for the US before the release of "Vivir Callados no es Vivir". Despite the movement of people out of Venezuela, Rojas says that punk bands that remain active tend to share musicians, and those who fled to neighboring places like Chile, Argentina, Colombia, and

Peru still represent their home within other bands. "It keeps the flame alive."

While that flame only flickers today, work is being done to revitalize the country's scene. "We are happy to do our part to help keep Venezuelan punk alive for the new generations," Rojas shares. "Although I will say there doesn't seem to be a lot of activity, and we know that it is not easy because there is fear. There are young people, however, speaking out through other musical genres, and that fills us with hope.

"We hope that in the future, the punk movement in Venezuela can reclaim its essence, which is to sing about the reality in Venezuela, as there is a lot to sing about."

Since the turn of the century, the world has seen numerous wars. The Iraq and Afghanistan wars, civil wars in Libya, South Sudan and Yemen throughout the 2010s, and now, with Russia's invasion of Ukraine, the outbreak of the Israel-Hamas war and growing unrest around the world – these barely scrape the surface. Millions of people have been displaced and innumerable lives lost or forever upended.

This is the reality of war. In writing this book and in having these conversations, it has underlined all the more that casualties aren't just body counts. Lives, livelihoods, down to the very concept of home, it's all at stake when the violence begins. When faced with this reality, some protest, some create, some merely want to survive to see another day, a better life. Music has been a means to achieve all of it, providing a voice with which to shout against or for something, an outlet to express, a vehicle for hope. Punk has been just one of the many forms of this, used to stand against war and oppression, but also for escape, for freedom, for the belief that there is a future worth fighting for, worth striving for together.

Something that at first had to be underground and covertly cultured, punk now exists proudly. Once shadowy figures, muffled messages and censored ideas are now being broadcast for the world to see and hear, inviting others to join them on their mission to make a difference and to keep alive the flame that these punks at war ignited.

Conclusion

"What is my crime exactly?" Nadya Tolokonnikova of Pussy Riot asks the audience in her TED Talk in April 2023. "I sang a song. 'Virgin Mary, Please Get Rid of Putin'."[130]

Since the invasion of Ukraine began in 2022, Russia's President Vladimir Putin and his actions have been condemned worldwide. Several Western nations responded by imposing strict sanctions on Russia, penalties that began by targeting the country's economy.[131] Anti-war protests broke out simultaneously around the globe, with daily demonstrations staged across Russia leading to thousands detained within the initial weeks of invasion,[132] a story of state repression all too common in the country, and all too familiar to a group like Pussy Riot.

For years, Pussy Riot have achieved global recognition for their bold activism and outspoken rejection of Putin's draconian regime, employing eye-catching tactics like flying Pride flags from Moscow's government buildings on Putin's birthday[133] – LGBTQ+ advocacy has been labeled as "extremist" in the country[134] – and using methods more combative.

Tolokonnikova and a handful of Pussy Riot's punk provocateurs performed "Virgin Mary, Please Get Rid of Putin" inside Moscow's Cathedral of Christ the Saviour, loudly proselytizing their punk doctrine in the holy place, in an event that would be remembered as their "Punk Prayer". Veiled in Day-Glo balaclavas, this style of protest continues to be Pussy Riot's modus operandi. "We would show up in public places, unannounced, guerrilla-style," Tolokonnikova tells the crowd. "No permits at all. And perform, preach. We performed in government buildings, squares, shopping malls, and we would get arrested almost every single day, get out and go back to action." This particular act in 2012, however, saw her and two other members arrested for "hooliganism motivated by religious hatred" and held as political prisoners for nearly two years in a Siberian penal colony.[135]

Their job, according to Nadya, was to "show the people of Russia that resisting is indeed an option." This is also the job of punk: to move people, to make them understand that resistance is not only possible; it can be imperative.

While punk's rebellious heart remains, beating defiantly against the years, the fads, the trends, punk has grown into more than just a sound or a style, bigger than a snarl and a shout. Today, it is in urgent demand. Whatever that may look like, be it mohawked and caped in leather or purely a fist raised in rebellion.

As the war in Ukraine progressed, another globe-quaking conflict erupted on October 7, 2023, when Hamas-led militant groups launched an attack on Israel near the Gaza Strip. The assault by land, air and sea resulted in more than 1,200 deaths, with some 250 more taken hostage. Hamas, or the Islamic Resistance Movement, [136] cited atrocities faced by Palestinians over years of Israeli occupation for their attack. Soon after this assault, Israeli forces responded with greater intensity, conducting air strikes and eventually a ground invasion. The Israel-Hamas war, which, at the time of writing, remains ongoing mainly in and around the Palestinian territory of Gaza, now targeting the former safe-zone Rafah, has resulted in the deaths of tens of thousands, with UN human rights expert Francesca Albanese subsequently declaring that Israel "is committing the crime of genocide against the Palestinians as a group in Gaza", a report the state has vehemently rejected. [137] [138]

Since fighting began, entire districts of Gaza City have been pummeled by Israeli bombardment, forcing a reported two million people from their homes. Those who remained in the devastated area, where houses, hospitals, water and sanitation facilities have been severely damaged if not destroyed, face desperate food and water insecurities with famine reportedly imminent. Humanitarian aid has slowed significantly due to continued attacks, movement restrictions and fuel short-ages.[139] While exact numbers are unknown, early 2024 reports estimated around 33,000 Palestinians, including more than 13,000 children, had been killed.[140]

Millions worldwide have spoken out against the violence, calling for a ceasefire, and, furthermore, the liberation of Palestine. Waves of protests were triggered, with an estimated 4,200 demonstrations taking place globally during the first weeks of the conflict.[141] In major U.S. cities like Los Angeles and Brooklyn, pro-Palestine punk shows were organized in response. These respective communities gathered en masse to show solidarity, raise awareness, and collect funds to aid those in the region.

Brooklyn's Herbert Von King Park hosted one such rally in support of a free Palestine. "As people living in this country, we have a specific responsibility because our government aids and abets this genocide and occu-pation," Sema Dayoub, one of the event's organizers, tells me, alluding to the United States' relationship with Israel, a longtime recipient of billions of dollars in U.S. foreign aid, a large portion of which benefits the state's military.[142] Their hardcore band Pure Terror headlined the show, which also saw performances from other local hardcore groups like Cross, No Knock, and Suck. "We wanted to educate and mobilize a community that is already huge and interconnected in so many ways."

"We also wanted to bring people together," they continue on the event, the efforts of which benefitted the Palestinian Youth Movement. "It's traumatic, especially for Palestinians and Arabs, to witness this happening to our people. I wanted to create an outlet for people to express their anger and grief and physically see this mass of people who are willing to come out for something like this."

Wielding cardboard signs that read "It's Not War, It's Genocide" or "No $$$ for Genocide" and waving the Palestinian flag, over 700 people filled the park's amphitheater with chanting – shouts like "thawra", Arabic for "revolution" – music, moshing, the sounds of resistance. They banded together, those personally connected to Palestine, and those not but seeing the inhumanity, to call out injustice and cry out for freedom and peace.[143]

"Punk culture and ideology is so hard to define because it has meant so many different things to so many different people," Sema explains. "I think a common thread is rebellion – which aligns very closely with resistance. Before we started our set, I led a chant that goes, 'Intifada, intifada, long live the intifada.' The word intifada means resistance, and resistance is beautiful."

Resistance *is* beautiful. It's powerful. It's an ember that's been aglow in every one of the conversations I've had, in every story I've been told or researched, over the last year of crafting this book. I've witnessed it crackle and spark in the songs of these punks, in their messages and in their fight, and I've studied how even the smallest flame can spread.

As long as there is conflict, oppression, and strife – as long as there is a need for resistance – punk will remain paramount. Because, in the end, it's about more than just music. Punk is more than just noise; it always has been, ever since it was gnawed and spat from the mouths of its forebears once addled by angst, dissatisfaction and a jones for something different, something better. Punk has come to stand for even more, a few shouted words and a hail of sound and fury bearing the ability to inspire change, incite action and ignite revolution.

Blitzkrieg Bops is a mere snapshot of those who have laid their lives on the line and fought via their music, to inspire others to stand with them, to dream of a better future. Knowing there are many more fighting today and likely many more battles still to come, Kyaw Kyaw's words return to me: The idea is the revolution. The idea, it never dies.

We cannot let it. Each song, each story, each revolution – we must keep it alive.

References

Introduction

1   "Notting Hill Carnival: Resistance and Protest." Notting Hill
       Carnival, *Google Arts & Culture*. artsandculture.google.com/
       story/notting-hill-carnival-resistance-and-protest/
       TAURrshcGWpLSA. Accessed 12 June 2024.
2   "The Story Behind The Song: 'White Riot' The Clash's
       misunderstood punk masterclass." Jack Whatley, *Far Out*,
       18 March 2021. faroutmagazine.co.uk/the-clash-strummer-
       white-riot-story-behind-the-song/. Accessed 12 June 2024.
3   "Ukrainian hardcore band Death Pill were working on their
       debut album. Then Russia invaded and their worlds turned
       upside down." Emily Swingle, *Metal Hammer*, 12 April 2023.
       loudersound.com/features/death-pill-band-ukraine-punk-
       russia-war. Accessed 12 June 2024.
4   "Here's what we know about how Russia's invasion of Ukraine
       unfolded." Tim Lister, Tara John, Paul P. Murphy, *CNN*, 24
       February 2022. cnn.com/2022/02/24/europe/ukraine-russia-
       attack-timeline-intl/index.html Accessed 12 June 2024.
5   "Refugees from Ukraine recorded in Europe." data.unhcr.org/
       en/situations/ukraine. Accessed 12 June 2024.
6   "Two civilian power plants seriously damaged in latest russian
       missile attack" *DTEK*, 1 June 2024. dtek.com/en/media-
       center/news/two-civilian-power-plants-seriously-dam-
       aged-in-latest-russian-missile-attack/. Accessed 12 June 2024.
7   "Why does the 1970s get painted as such a bad decade?"
       BBC, 16 April 2012. bbc.com/news/magazine-17703483.
       Accessed 12 June 2024.

Chapter 1

8   "Unemployment rate in the United Kingdom from March 1971 to April 2024." *Statista*. statista.com/statistics/279898/ unemployment-rate-in-the-united-kingdom-uk/. Accessed 12 June 2024.

9   "Historical U.S. Unemployment Rate by Year." Nathan Reiff, *Investopedia*, 17 October 2023. investopedia.com/ historical-us-unemployment-rate-by-year-7495494. Accessed 12 June 2024.

10   "Oil Shock of 1973–74." Michael Corbett, Federal Reserve History. federalreservehistory.org/essays/oil-shock-of-1973-74. Accessed 12 June 2024.

11   "1979 Energy Crisis: Definition, History, Causes, and Impact." Lucas Downey, Investopedia, 14 July 2022. investopedia.com/terms/1/1979-energy-crisis.asp. Accessed 12 June 2024.

12   "Racial Tension in the 1970s." *The White House Historical Ascocation*. whitehousehistory.org/racial-tension-in-the-1970s. Accessed 12 June 2024.

13   "Gay Rights." *History*, 28 June 2017. history.com/topics/ gay-rights/history-of-gay-rights. Accessed 12 June 2024.

14   "The early battle for women's rights in the UK." J&P, 1 March 2024. judge-priestley.co.uk/site/news/articles/ the-early-battle-for-womens-rights-in-the-uk. Accessed 12 June 2024.

15   "Anarchy Around The World: Punk Goes Global." Tim Peacock, *udiscovermusic*, 24 January 2024. udiscovermusic. com/in-depth-features/anarchy-around-the-world-punk-goes-global/. Accessed 12 June 2024.

16   "Total number of deaths per year during the Troubles (the Northern Ireland Conflict) from 1969 to 2001." *Statista*. statista.com/statistics/1401907/ni-troubles-deaths-annual/. Accessed 12 June 2024.

17   "1976: Ten dead in Northern Ireland ambush." *BBC*. news.bbc.co.uk/onthisday/hi/dates/stories/january/5/ newsid_2500000/2500393.stm. Accessed 12 June 2024.

18   "Murdered by the Glenanne gang: 'Patrick lived till the ripe old age of 13'." Susan McKay, *Irish Times*, 2 May 2015.

irishtimes.com/news/crime-and-law/murdered-by-
the-glenanne-gang-patrick-lived-till-the-ripe-old-
age-of-13-1.2197148. Accessed 12 June 2024.

19 "What were the Troubles that ravaged Northern Ireland?"
Erin Blakemore, National Geographic, 8 April 2022.
nationalgeographic.com/history/article/the-troubles-of-
northern-ireland-history. Accessed 12 June 2024.

20 "How punk acted as a peacemaker for youth in Northern
Ireland." Niall Flynn, Dazed, 22 September 2017.
dazeddigital.com/art-photography/article/37456/1/how-
punk-acted-as-a-peacemaker-for-youth-in-northern-ireland.
Accessed 12 June 2024.

21 "Alternative Ulster: how punk took on the Troubles." Timothy Heron, *Irish Times*, 2 December 2016. irishtimes.com/
culture/books/alternative-ulster-how-punk-took-on-the-
troubles-1.2890644. Accessed 12 June 2024.

22 "'Bloody Friday' - Summary of Main Events." Martin
Melaugh, *CAIN Web Service*. cain.ulster.ac.uk/events/bfriday/
sum.htm. Accessed 12 June 2024.

23 Ibid.

24 "Total number of deaths per year during the Troubles (the
Northern Ireland Conflict) from 1969 to 2001." *Statista*.
statista.com/statistics/1401907/ni-troubles-deaths-annual/.
Accessed 12 June 2024.

25 "The Undertones: 'We never wanted to sing about the Troubles – we sang to get girls'." Ian Winwood, *The Telegraph*, 16
March 2022. telegraph.co.uk/music/interviews/undertones-
never-wanted-sing-troubles-sang-get-girls/. Accessed 12 June
2024.

26 "Alternative Ulster: how punk took on the Troubles." Ibid.

27 "Fact Sheet on the conflict in and about Northern Ireland."
cain.ulster.ac.uk/victims/docs/group/htr/day_of_reflection/
htr_0607c.pdf. Accessed 12 June 2024.

28 "Legacy of the Troubles still haunts Northern Ireland." Peter
Geoghegan, *Politico*, 30 March 2018. politico.eu/article/
northern-ireland-troubles-legacy-good-friday-agreement/.
Accessed 12 June 2024.

29 "The heavy toll of the Troubles on brain health in North-

ern Ireland." *Trinity College Dublin*, 19 April 2023. tcd.ie/
news_events/articles/2023/the-heavy-toll-of-the-troubles-on-
the-brain-health-of-people-in-northern-ireland/. Accessed 12
June 2024.

30 "Legacy of the Troubles still haunts Northern Ireland." Ibid.

31 "apartheid." *Cornell Law School*. law.cornell.edu/wex/
apartheid. Accessed 12 June 2024.

32 "A Look Back at South Africa Under Apartheid, Twenty-Five
Years After Its Repeal." Katie Nodjimbadem, *Smithsonian
Magazine*, 15 October 2015. smithsonianmag.com/history/
what-did-apartheid-south-africa-look-180956945/.
Accessed 12 June 2024.

33 "How did Apartheid happen, and how did it finally end?"
Thula Simpson, *TED*, December 2023. ted.com/talks/
thula_simpson_how_did_apartheid_happen_and_how_did_
it_finally_end. Accessed 12 June 2024.

34 "South Africa's struggle songs against apartheid come from a
long tradition of resistance." Sisanda Nkoala, *The Conversa-
tion*, 20 October 2022. theconversation.com/south-africas-
struggle-songs-against-apartheid-come-from-a-long-
tradition-of-resistance-192425. Accessed 12 June 2024.

35 "National Wake: the South African punk band who defied
apartheid." Alexis Petridis, *The Guardian*, 3 October 2013.
theguardian.com/music/2013/oct/03/national-wake-south-
africa-punk-apartheid. Accessed 12 June 2024.

36 "Avant-(Ap)art(heid): South African Protest Punk in a
Dangerous Time." Carl Wilson, *Hazlit*, 10 December 2013.
hazlitt.net/feature/avant-apartheid-south-african-protest-
punk-dangerous-time. Accessed 12 June 2024.

37 James Greene, *Brave Punk World: The International Rock
Underground from Alerta Roja to Z-Off*. Rowman & Little-
field, 2017. pg. 253 – 256.

38 "National Wake." *Light in the Attic*. lightintheattic.net/
collections/national-wake. Accessed 12 June 2024.

39 Ibid.

40 "National Wake: the South African punk band who defied
apartheid." Ibid.

Chapter 2

41   "Cold Conflict." *The National WWII Museum.* nationalww2museum.org/war/articles/cold-conflict. Accessed 12 June 2024.

42   "The Allende Years and the Pinochet Coup, 1969–1973." *Office of the Historian.* history.state.gov/milestones/1969-1976/allende. Accessed 12 June 2024.

43   "The U.S. set the stage for a coup in Chile. It had unintended consequences at home." James Doubek, *NPR*, 10 September 2023. npr.org/2023/09/10/1193755188/chile-coup-50-years-pinochet-kissinger-human-rights-allende. Accessed 12 June 2024.

44   "Life under Punochet: 'The day we buried our freedom'." *Amnesty International,* 11 September 2013. amnesty.org/es/wp-content/uploads/2021/06/amr220122013en.pdf. Accessed 12 June 2024.

45   "'A fascist tried to electrocute us on stage': the musicians who took on the Chilean junta." Naomi Larsson Piñeda, *The Guardian*, 11 September 2023. theguardian.com/music/2023/sep/11/music-pinochet-allende-hacia-la-victoria-chile-politics-resistance. Accessed 12 June 2024.

46   "The last days of Víctor Jara: Chile's political poet killed by the Pinochet dictatorship." Ana María Sanhueza, *El Pais*, 28 February 2023. english.elpais.com/international/2023-02-28/the-last-days-of-victor-jara-chiles-political-poet-killed-by-the-pinochet-dictatorship.html. Accessed 12 June 2024.

47   "A Very Brief History of Punk in Chile." *DIY Conspiracy*, 21 February 2019. diyconspiracy.net/a-very-brief-history-of-punk-in-chile/. Accessed 12 June 2024.

48   Ibid.

49   "Chile's 1988 Plebiscite and the End of Pinochet's Dictatorship." *Assocation for Diplomatic Studies and Training*. adst.org/2014/11/chiles-1988-plebiscite-and-the-end-of-pinochets-dictatorship/. Accessed 12 June 2024.

50   "What was the Berlin Wall and how did it fall?" *IWN*. iwm.org.uk/history/what-was-the-berlin-wall-and-how-did-it-fall. Accessed 12 June 2024.

51   "East Germany." *The Atlantic*, October 1961. theatlantic.com/magazine/archive/1961/10/east-germany/658346/.

Accessed 12 June 2024.

52   "Border zones: 'Berlin in the 1980s was like an advert
      for hedonism'." Chris Petit, The Guardian, 12 July 2016.
      theguardian.com/film/2016/jul/12/how-berlin-made-me-a-
      better-artist-chris-petit. Accessed 12 June 2024.

53   "EAST GERMANY." *Alpha History*. alphahistory.com/
      coldwar/east-germany. Accessed 12 June 2024.

54   "German Democratic Republic: Youth Movement." *Historical
      Boys' Unifrom*. histclo.com/youth/youth/org/pio/pioneerg.
      htm. Accessed 12 June 2024.

55   "Freedom, Restriction and Coded Language." Goethe-
      Institut New York, *YouTube*, 30 November 2022. youtube.
      com/watch?v=GluQRAUfbRo. Accessed 12 June 2024.

56   "The East German punks who helped bring down the Berlin
      Wall." April Clare Welsh, *Dazed*, 7 November 2019.
      dazeddigital.com/music/article/46734/1/east-german-punks-
      fall-of-berlin-wall-30th-anniversary. Accessed 12 June 2024.

57   "Punk persecution: how East Germany cracked down on
      alternative lifestyles." *The Guardian*, 5 November 2019.
      theguardian.com/world/gallery/2019/nov/05/punk-
      persecution-east-germany-stasi-secret-police-in-pictures.
      Accessed 12 June 2024.

58   "The East German punks who helped bring down the Berlin
      Wall." Ibid.

59   "Punk persecution: how East Germany cracked down on
      alternative lifestyles." Ibid.

60   "This is the true story of the Stasi's brutal crackdown on East
      German punk music." Tim Mohr, *GQ*, 28 September 2019.
      gq-magazine.co.uk/culture/article/burning-down-the-haus-
      tim-mohr-extract. Accessed 12 June 2024.

61   "What is open youth work?" *BOJA*. boja.at/was-ist-offene-
      jugendarbeit. Accessed 12 June 2024.

62   "Punk persecution: how East Germany cracked down on
      alternative lifestyles." Ibid.

63   "The East German punks who helped bring down the Berlin
      Wall." Ibid.

64   "The Peaceful Revolution: The Fall of a Wall and the Rise
      of Democracy." Cindy Barbosa, The Nonviolence Project, 4

February 2024. thenonviolenceproject.wisc.edu/2024/02/04/the-peaceful-revolution-the-fall-of-a-wall-and-the-rise-of-democracy/. Accessed 12 June 2024.

65   "Fall of Berlin Wall: How 1989 reshaped the modern world." *BBC*, 5 November 2019. bbc.com/news/world-europe-50013048. Accessed 12 June 2024.

66   "What really happened in the 1989 Tiananmen Square protests." *Amnesty International*. amnesty.org.uk/china-1989-tiananmen-square-protests-demonstration-massacre. Accessed 12 June 2024.

67   "Anarchy Around The World: Punk Goes Global." Ibid.

Chapter 3

68   "1989 Revolutions." *Miami University*. miamioh.edu/cas/centers-institutes/havighurst-center/additional-resources/havighurst-special-programming/1989-revolutions/index.html. Accessed 12 June 2024.

69   "Fall of Communism in Eastern Europe, 1989." *Office of the Historian*. history.state.gov/milestones/1989-1992/fall-of-communism. Accessed 12 June 2024.

70   "13. TECHNOLOGY AND CULTURE." *UEN*. uen.pressbooks.pub/tech1010/chapter/technology-and-culture. Accessed 12 June 2024.

71   "Anarchy in the E.U: the history of punk in Yugoslavia." Jelena Prtorić, *Europavox*, 5 May 2017. europavox.com/news/anarchy-e-u-history-punk-yugoslavia/. Accessed 12 June 2024.

72   "YUGOSLAV PUNK: AN INTRODUCTION." yugoslavpunk.omeka.net/exhibits/show/intro/yugoslav-punk--an-introduction. Accessed 12 June 2024.

73   "A Slow Burning Fire: The Rise of the New Art Practice in Yugoslavia." Adair Rounthwaite, *ArtMargins*, 17 January 2022. artmargins.com/a-slow-burning-fire-the-rise-of-the-new-art-practice-in-yugoslavia/#ftn_artnotes1_1. Accessed 12 June 2024.

74   "Belgrade's 1968 student unrest spurs nostalgia." *Thaindian News*. web.archive.org/web/20161230085545/http://www.thaindian.com/newsportal/world-news/belgrades-1968-

student-unrest-spurs-nostalgia_10056711.html. Accessed 12 June 2024.

75   "CENSORSHIP IN THE AGE OF PUNK: YUGOSLAVIA 1970-1989." yugoslavpunk.omeka.net/exhibits/show/censorship/censorship-in-the-age-of-punk-. Accessed 12 June 2024.

76   "PUNK IN PRINT: PUBLICIZING YUGOSLAV PUNK AND ROCK." yugoslavpunk.omeka.net/exhibits/show/publications/publications. Accessed 12 June 2024.

77   "The Future is Between Your Legs: Sex, Art and Censorship in the Socialist Federal Republic of Yugoslavia." *faktogradia.com.* faktografia.com/2015/09/06/the-future-is-between-your-legs-sex-art-and-censorship-in-the-socialist-federal-republic-of-yugoslavia/. Accessed 12 June 2024.

78   "CENSORSHIP IN THE AGE OF PUNK: YUGOSLAVIA 1970-1989." Ibid.

79   "The Breakup of Yugoslavia, 1990–1992." *Office of the Historian.* history.state.gov/milestones/1989-1992/breakup-yugoslavia. Accessed 12 June 2024.

80   "The Breakup of Yugoslavia." *Remembering Srebrenica.* srebrenica.org.uk/what-happened/history/breakup-yugoslavia. Accessed 12 June 2024.

81   "History of Ethnic Tensions." *United States Holocaust Memorial Museum.* ushmm.org/genocide-prevention/countries/bosnia-herzegovina/history-ethnic-tensions. Accessed 12 June 2024.

82   As cited in Svanibor Pettan's introduction of Music, Politics, and War in Croatia in the 1990s, https://www.ag.uni-lj.si/e_files/zaposleni_datoteke/73/MUSIC,POLITICS%20AND%20WAR.pdf P14. Accessed 12 June 2024.

83   "30th anniversary of iconic Croatian song 'Moja domovina' to be marked with documentary film." *Croatioa Week,* 15 September 2021. https://www.croatiaweek.com/30th-anniversary-of-iconic-croatian-song-moja-domovina-to-be-marked-with-documentary-film/. Accessed 12 June 2024.

84   "Anti-war and peace ideas in the history of Serbia and anti-war movements until the year 2000." republika.co.rs/492-493/20.html. Accessed 12 June 2024.

85 "The Unbearable Lightness of Going to War." *forumZFD*. forumzfd.de/en/unbearable-lightness-going-war. Accessed 12 June 2024.

86 "The 1990s Balkan Wars in Key Dates." *AFP*. voanews.com/a/timeline-of-balkan-wars/4129662.html. Accessed 12 June 2024.

87 "Civilians bore the brunt of 1,425-day Sarajevo siege." *Genocide Watch*. genocidewatch.com/single-post/civilians-bore-the-brunt-of-1-425-day-sarajevo-siege. Accessed 12 June 2024.

88 "Genocide in Bosnia." *Holocaust Museum Houston*. hmh.org/library/research/genocide-in-bosnia-guide/. Accessed 12 June 2024.

89 "Just Another Day in a Besieged City," a 2022 personal essay published by the platform Kosovo 2.0. kosovotwopointzero.com/en/just-another-day-in-a-besieged-city/. Accessed 12 June 2024.

90 Ibid.

91 "Ceasefire Agreement for Bosnia and Herzegovina." pax. peaceagreements.org/agreements/322/. Accessed 12 June 2024.

92 "The Second Intifada: Background and Causes of the Israeli-Palestinian Conflict." Jeremy Pressman, 2003. journals.lib.unb.ca/index.php/jcs/article/view/220/378. Accessed 12 June 2024.

93 "Religion and the Israel-Palestinian Conflict: Cause, Consequence, and Cure." Mohamed Galal Mostafa, Washington Institute, 31 May 2018. washingtoninstitute.org/policy-analysis/religion-and-israel-palestinian-conflict-cause-consequence-and-cure. Accessed 12 June 2024.

94 "What were the intifadas?" Zack Beauchamp, *Vox*, 14 May 2018. vox.com/2018/11/20/18080066/israel-palestine-intifadas-first-second. Accessed 12 June 2024.

95 Orlando Crowcroft, *Rock in a Hard Place: Music and Mayhem in the Middle East*. Zed Books, 2017. p196 – 197.

96 "Interview with Filmmaker Liz Nord." *PBS*. pbs.org/frontline world/dispatches/israel/nord.html. Accessed 12 June 2024.

97 Ibid.

98 "The Zapatista Movement: The Fight for Indigenous Rights

in Mexico." Iker Reyes Godelmann, *Australian Institute of International Affairs*, 30 July 2014. internationalaffairs.org.au/news-item/the-zapatista-movement-the-fight-for-indigenous-rights-in-mexico/. Accessed 12 June 2024.

99   "Anarchy Around The World: Punk Goes Global." Ibid.

Chapter 4

100   "Great Recession: What It Was and What Caused It." *Investopedia*, 18 December 2023. investopedia.com/terms/g/great-recession.asp. Accessed 12 June 2024.

101   "London bombings of 2005." *British Transport Police*. btp.police.uk/police-forces/british-transport-police/areas/about-us/about-us/our-history/london-bombings-of-2005/. Accessed 12 June 2024.

102   "Burmese (Myanmar) monks campaign for democracy (Saffron Revolution), 2007." *Global Nonviolent Action Database*. nvdatabase.swarthmore.edu/content/burmese-myanmar-monks-campaign-democracy-saffron-revolution-2007. Accessed 12 June 2024.

103   "Myanmar's Saffron Revolution: 10 Years Later." rfa.org/english/news/special/saffron/. Accessed 12 June 2024.

104   "The Geopolitics And Economics Of Burma's Military Regime, 1962-2007. Understanding SPDC Tyranny." Donald M. Seekins, *Asia-Pacific Journal*, 3 November 2007. apjjf.org/donald-m-seekins/2573/article. Accessed 12 June 2024.

105   "Myanmar's Saffron Revolution: 10 Years Later." Ibid.

106   "Burmese (Myanmar) monks campaign for democracy (Saffron Revolution), 2007." Ibid.

107   "Repression of the 2007 Popular Protests in Burma." *Human Rights Watch*. hrw.org/report/2007/12/06/crackdown/repression-2007-popular-protests-burma. Accessed 12 June 2024.

108   "Buddhist monk rally steps up pressure on Burma's junta." Jonathan Watts, *The Guardian*, 20 September 2007. theguardian.com/world/2007/sep/20/burma.jonathanwatts. Accessed 12 June 2024.

109   "Burmese (Myanmar) monks campaign for democracy (Saffron Revolution), 2007." Ibid.

110   Ibid.

111 "Repression of the 2007 Popular Protests in Burma." Ibid.

112 rfa.org/english/news/special/saffron/. Accessed 12 June 2024.

113 unodc.org/docs/treatment/CoPro/Web_Myanmar.pdf. Accessed 12 June 2024.

114 foodnotbombs.net/new_site/. Accessed 12 June 2024.

115 "Myanmar junta blocks internet access as coup protests expand." *AP*, 1 February 2021. apnews.com/article/united-nations-myanmar-media-social-media-yangon-e7765d3459d386219ee1dca8ad1e089c. Accessed 12 June 2024.

116 "To... Dear Comrade." therebelriot.bandcamp.com/album/to-dear-comrade. Accessed 12 June 2024.

117 "Ras Al Ghul - Catching stars (refugee song)." Ras Al Ghul DXB, *YouTube*, 25 September 2017. youtu.be/7kHJ7nn2td8. Accessed 12 June 2024.

118 "Oppression, harrasment and escape – An inside story of metal in Syria." *Barametal.* barametal.wordpress.com/2015/10/22/oppression-harrasment-and-escape-an-inside-story-of-metal-in-syria/. Accessed 12 June 2024.

119 "Syria's Civil War: The Descent Into Horror." *Council on Foreign Relations*, 14 February 2023. cfr.org/article/syrias-civil-war. Accessed 12 June 2024.

120 "The Syrian Regime Legal "Reforms" (II)" State of Emergency as the Trojan Horse of Counter-Terrorism." Nael Georges, *The Legal Agenda*, 26 December 2013. english.legal-agenda.com/the-syrian-regime-legal-reforms-ii-state-of-emergency-as-the-trojan-horse-of-counter-terrorism/. Accessed 12 June 2024.

121 "Syria protests: Assad to lift state of emergency." *BBC*, 20 April 2011. bbc.com/news/world-middle-east-13134322. Accessed 12 June 2024.

122 "Syria Refugee Crisis Explained." *UNHCR*, 13 March 2024. unrefugees.org/news/syria-refugee-crisis-explained/. Accessed 12 June 2024.

123 "Reviving Venezuelan Punk, the Music of Revolution." Camila Osorio, *The New Yorker*, 20 October 2019. newyorker.com/culture/culture-desk/reviving-venezuelan-punk-the-music-of-revolution. Accessed 12 June 2024.

124 "#LiberenAJoséMendoza Porque la promoción cultural y la

libertad de expresión no son delito. #20Sept."
@Uladdhh, *X*, 20 September 2019. https://x.com/Uladdhh/
status/1175070317754163200. Accessed 12 June 2024.

125 "Ministro: ¿Cuál es su trabajo?" humanoderechorecords.
bandcamp.com/album/ministro-cu-l-es-su-trabajo.
Accessed 12 June 2024.

126 "Venezuela: The Rise and Fall of a Petrostate." Amelia
Cheatham, Diana Roy, *Council on Foreign Relations*, 22
December 2023. cfr.org/backgrounder/venezuela-crisis.
Accessed 12 June 2024.

127 "Venezuela: Inflation rate from 1985 to 2025." *Statista*.
statista.com/statistics/371895/inflation-rate-in-venezuela/.
Accessed 12 June 2024.

128 "Venezuela crisis in brief." Vanessa Buschschlüter *BBC*, 31
January. https://www.bbc.com/news/world-latin-
america-48121148. Accessed 12 June 2024.

129 "Venezuela Crisis Explained." *UNHCR*, 17 April 2024.
unrefugees.org/news/venezuela-crisis-explained/.
Accessed 12 June 2024.

Conclusion

130 "Pussy Riot's powerful message to Vladimir Putin." Nadya
Tolokonnikova, *TED*, April 2023. ted.com/talks/nadya_
tolokonnikova_pussy_riot_s_powerful_message_to_
vladimir_putin. Accessed 12 June 2024.

131 "Russia faces financial meltdown as sanctions slam its economy." Mark Thompson, Anna Chernova, Vasco Cotovio,
CNN, 28 February 2022. edition.cnn.com/2022/02/28/
business/russia-ruble-banks-sanctions/index.html.
Accessed 12 June 2024.

132 "Thousands have been detained in anti-war protests across
Russia." Jonathan Franklin, *NPR*, 6 March 2022. npr.
org/2022/03/06/1084818519/russia-protests-detainments.
Accessed 12 June 2024.

133 "Pussy Riot Flies LGBT Flags From Gov't Buildings to
Mark Putin's Birthday." *The Moscow Times*, 7 October 2020.
themoscowtimes.com/2020/10/07/pussy-riot-flies-lgbt-
flags-from-govt-buildings-to-mark-putins-birthday-a71680.

Accessed 12 June 2024.

134 "On the Run With Pussy Riot." Casey Quackenbush, *Intelligencer*, 13 December 2023. nymag.com/
intelligencer/2023/12/pussy-riot-on-the-run-from-
vladimir-putin.html. Accessed 12 June 2024.

135 "Pussy Riot's Punk Prayer is pure protest poetry." Carol
Rumens, *The Guardian*, 20 August 2012. theguardian.com/
books/2012/aug/20/pussy-riot-punk-prayer-lyrics.
Accessed 12 June 2024.

136 "What is Hamas and why is it fighting with Israel in Gaza?"
BBC, 5 April 2024. bbc.com/news/world-
middle-east-67039975. Accessed 12 June 2024.

137 "Gaza war: UN rights expert accuses Israel of acts of genocide." *BBC*, 26 March 2024. bbc.co.uk/news/world-
middle-east-68667556. Accessed 12 June 2024.

138 "'Reasonable grounds' to believe Israel is committing genocide in Gaza, UN rights expert says." Louis Mian, Benjamin
Brown, *CNN*, 27 March 2024. cnn.com/2024/03/27/
middleeast/israel-committing-genocide-in-gaza-un-rights-
expert-says-intl/index.html. Accessed 12 June 2024.

139 "Gaza Strip in maps: How life has changed." *BBC*, 22 March
2024. bbc.com/news/world-middle-east-20415675. Accessed
12 June 2024.

140 "Half a year into the war in Gaza, here's a look at the conflict
by the numbers." Julia Frankel, *AP*, 6 April 2024. apnews.
com/article/israel-hamas-gaza-war-statistics-95a6407f
ac94e9d589be234708cd5005. Accessed 12 June 2024.

141 "Infographic: Global Demonstrations in Response to the Isra-
el-Palestine Conflict." Timothy Lay, Ciro Murillo, *ACLED*,
7 November 2023. acleddata.com/2023/11/07/infographic-
global-demonstrations-in-response-to-the-israel-palestine-
conflict/. Accessed 12 June 2024.

142 "U.S. Aid to Israel in Four Charts." Jonathan Masters, Will
Merrow, *Council on Foreign Relations*, 31 May 2024. cfr.org/
article/us-aid-israel-four-charts. Accessed 12 June 2024.

143 "SCENES FROM A PRO-PALESTINE HARDCORE
SHOW IN BED-STUY." Stephanie Keith, *Brooklyn*, 13
November 2023. bkmag.com/2023/11/13/scenes-from-a-
pro-palestine-hardcore-show-in-bed-stuy/. Accessed 12 June
2024.

Acknowledgements

First, thank you to the publishers of 404 Ink, Heather McDaid and Laura Jones-Rivera, for believing in this idea and for your commitment to little books that need to be read. Also, Heather, your guidance throughout the editorial process made this book what it is, and I can't thank you enough for your insight. Thank you to Dr Vladislav Beronja for your invaluable expertise. Thank you to Orlando Crowcroft for your time and for your indispensable book. Thank you, BeShaun Leavell, for sharing your experiences with me. Thank you to Annika Freund and Nicholas Castro Price for your translation assistance; your help made telling many of these stories possible. "Thank you" doesn't come close to expressing my appreciation for Ethan Curry, who, even on my worst days, is my biggest cheerleader.

But, most of all, I want to express my deepest gratitude to all the punks who made this book a reality. I could not have written a word of it without, first, your bravery and, second, your willingness to share your stories with me. Thank you, Mariana Navrotskaya, Natalya Seryakova, Anastasiya Khomenko, Ali McMordie, Ivan and Nadine Kadey, Daniel Puente Encina and Astrid-Maren Bormann, Jana Schlosser, Dario "Adam" Adamic, Srđan Gojković "Gile", Yotam Ben Horin, Guy Carmel, Rashwan Zaza, Ernesto "Cuerdas Duras" Rojas, Kyaw Kyaw and the Rebel Riot community, and Sema Dayoub. I would need many more pages to fully convey how you've all inspired me. I will carry your stories and your songs with me always.

About the Author

Alli Patton is a writer and music journalist based in the American South. A lover of music, the written word, and combining the two, her work can be found in *The Independent*, *Holler*, and *American Songwriter*. She believes, above all things, in the power music has to bring about change.

About the Inklings series

This book is part of 404 Ink's Inkling series which presents big ideas in pocket-sized books.

They are all available at 404ink.com/shop.

If you enjoyed this book, you may also enjoy these titles in the series:

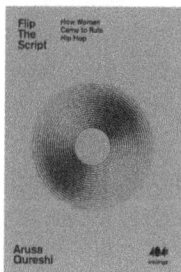

Flip the Script – Arusa Qureshi

Flip the Script explores the women who have paved the way in UK hip hop both at the forefront and behind the scenes, from the influence of the genre's beginnings in the Bronx to formation of distinctive regional scenes across the country.

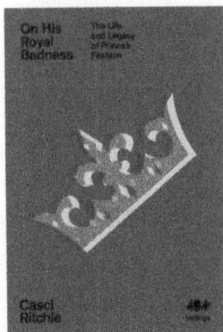

On His Royal Badness – Casci Ritchie

Taking core pieces from his wardrobe, Casci Ritchie embarks on a greatest hits compilation of how the simplest pieces can tell the most incredible stories, and how they act as their own marker for Prince's career and surrounding cultural impact.

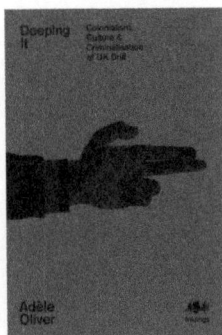

Deeping It – Adèle Oliver

Deeping It shines a critical light on UK drill and its fraught relationship with the British legal system. Intervening on current discourse steeped in anti-Blackness and moral panic, this Inkling 'deeps' how the criminalisation of UK drill cannot be disentangled from histories, technologies, and realities of colonialism, consumerism and more.